THE

PRAIRIE TRAVELER

THE

PRAIRIE TRAVELER

A HAND-BOOK
FOR
OVERLAND EXPEDITIONS.

WITH ILLUSTRATIONS, AND ITINERARIES OF

THE PRINCIPAL ROUTES BETWEEN THE

MISSISSIPPI AND THE PACIFIC,

AND A MAP.

BY RANDOLPH B. MARCY,

CAPTAIN U. S. AHMY.
(NOW GENERAL MARCY, CHIEF OF STAFF, ARMY OF THE POTOMAC.)

EDITED (WITH NOTES) BY

RICHARD F. BURTON, F.R.G.S.,

ETC.

ISBN: 978-93-5128-961-6(HB)

First Published in 1863
Indian Reprint in 2017

Published by

Kalpaz Publications
C-30, Satyawati Nagar,
Delhi – 110052
E-mail: kalpaz@hotmail.com
Website: kalpazpublications.com
Ph.: +91-9212142040

CONTENTS.

CHAPTER IV.

CHAPTER V.

CHAPTER VI.

CHAPTER VII.

LIST OF ILLUSTRATIONS.

PREFACE.

A QUARTER of a century's experience in frontier life, a great portion of which has been occupied in exploring the interior of our continent, and in long marches where I have been thrown exclusively upon my own resources, far beyond the bounds of the populated districts, and where the traveler must vary his expedients to surmount the numerous obstacles which the nature of the country continually reproduces, has shown me under what great disadvantages the *voyageur* labors for want of a timely initiation into those minor details of prairie-craft, which, however apparently unimportant in the abstract, are sure, upon the plains, to turn the balance of success for or against an enterprise.

This information is so varied, and is derived from so many different sources, that I still find every new expedition adds substantially to my practical knowledge, and am satisfied that a good Prairie Manual will be for the young traveler an addition to his equipment of inappreciable value.

With such a book in his hand, he will be able, in difficult circumstances, to avail himself of the matured experience of veteran travelers, and thereby avoid many otherwise unforeseen disasters; while, during the ordinary routine of marching, he will greatly augment the sum of his comforts, avoid many serious losses, and enjoy a comparative exemption from doubts and anxieties. He will feel himself a master spirit in the wilderness he traverses, and not the victim of every new combination of circumstances which nature affords or fate allots, as if to try his skill and prowess.

I have waited for several years, with the confident expectation that someone more competent than myself would assume the task, and give the public the desired information; but it seems that no one has taken sufficient interest in the subject to disseminate the benefits of his experience in this way. Our frontiersmen, although brave in council and action, and possessing an intelligence that quickens in the face of danger, are apt to feel shy of the pen. They shun the atmosphere of the student's closet; their sphere is in the free and open wilderness. It is not to be wondered at, therefore, that to our veteran borderer the field of literature should remain a *terra incognita.* It is our army that unites the chasm between the culture of civilization in the aspect of science, art, and social refinement, and the powerful simplicity of nature. On leaving the Military Academy, a majority of our officers are attached to the line of the army, and forthwith assigned to duty upon our remote and extended frontier, where the restless and warlike habits of the nomadic tribes render the soldier's life almost as unsettled as that of the savages themselves.

A regiment is stationed today on the borders of tropical Mexico; tomorrow, the war whoop, borne on a gale from the northwest, compels its presence in the frozen latitudes of Puget's Sound. The very limited numerical strength of our army, scattered as it is over a vast area of territory, necessitates constant changes of stations, long and toilsome marches, a promptitude of action, and a tireless energy and self-reliance, that can only be acquired through an intimate acquaintance with the sphere in which we act and move.

The education of our officers at the Military Academy is doubtless well adapted to the art of civilized warfare, but cannot familiarize them with the diversified details of border service; and they often, at the outset of their military career, find themselves compelled to improvise new expedients to meet novel emergences.

The life of the wilderness is an *art* as well as that of the city or court, and every art subjects its votaries to discipline in preparing them for a successful career in its pursuit. The Military Art, as enlarged to meet all the requirements of border service, the savage in his wiles or the elements in their caprices, embraces many other special arts which have hitherto been almost ignored, and results which experience and calculation should have guaranteed have been improvidently staked upon favorable chances.

PREFACE

The main object at which I have aimed in the following pages has been to explain and illustrate, as clearly and succinctly as possible, the best methods of performing the duties devolving upon the prairie traveler, so as to meet their contingencies under all circumstances, and thereby to endeavor to establish a more uniform system of marching and campaigning in the Indian country.

I have also given some information concerning the habits of the Indians and wild animals that frequent the prairies, with the secrets of the hunter's and warrior's strategy, which I have endeavored to impress more forcibly upon the reader by introducing illustrative anecdote.

I take great pleasure in acknowledging my indebtedness to several officers of the Topographical Engineers and of other corps of the army for the valuable information I have obtained from their official reports, and to these gentlemen I beg leave very respectfully to dedicate my book.

CHAPTER I.

The different Routes to California and Oregon.—Their respective Advantages. —Organization of Companies. —Elections of Captains. —Wagons and Teams. —Relative Merits of Mules and Oxen.—Stores and Provisions.—How packed.—Desiccated and canned Vegetables.—Pemmican.—Anti-scorbutics. —Cold Flour. —Substitutes in case of Necessity. —Amount of Supplies. —Clothing. —Camp Equipage.—Arms.

ROUTES TO CALIFORNIA AND OREGON.

EMIGRANTS or others desiring to make the overland journey to the Pacific should bear in mind that there are several different routes which may be traveled with wagons, each having its advocates in persons directly or indirectly interested in attracting the tide of emigration and travel over them.

Information concerning these routes coming from strangers living or owning property near them, from agents of steamboats or railways, or from other persons connected with transportation companies, should be received with great caution, and never without corroborating evidence from disinterested sources.

There is no doubt that each one of these roads has its advantages and disadvantages, but a judicious selection must depend chiefly upon the following considerations, namely, the locality from whence the individual is to take his departure, the season of the year when he desires to commence his journey, the character of his means of transportation, and the point upon the Pacific coast that he wishes to reach.

Persons living in the Northeastern States can, with about equal facility and dispatch, reach the eastern terminus of any one of the routes they may select by means of public transport. And, as animals are much cheaper upon the frontier than in the Eastern States, they should purchase their teams at or near the point where the overland journey is to commence.

Those living in the Northwestern States, having their own teams, and wishing to go to any point north of San Francisco, will of course make choice of the route which takes its departure from the Missouri River.

Those who live in the middle Western States, having their own means of transportation, and going to any point upon the Pacific coast, should take one of the middle routes.

Others, who reside in the extreme Southwest, and whose destination is south of San Francisco, should travel the southern road running through Texas, which is the only one practicable for comfortable winter travel. The grass upon a great portion of this route is green during the entire winter, and snow seldom covers it. This road leaves the Gulf coast at

Powder-horn, on Matagorda Bay, which point is difficult of access by land from the north, but may be reached by steamers from New Orleans five times a week.

There are stores at Powder-horn and Indianola where the traveler can obtain most of the articles necessary for his journey, but I would recommend him to supply himself before leaving New Orleans with everything he requires with the exception of animals, which he will find cheaper in Texas.

This road has received a large amount of travel since 1849, is well tracked and defined, and, excepting about twenty miles of "hog wallow prairie" near Powder-horn, it is an excellent road for carriages and wagons. It passes through a settled country for 250 miles, and within this section supplies can be had at reasonable rates.

At Victoria and San Antonio many fine stores will be found, well supplied with large stocks of goods, embracing all the articles the traveler will require.

The next route to the north is that over which the semiweekly mail to California passes, and which, for a great portion of the way to New Mexico, I traveled and recommended in 1849. This road leaves the Arkansas River at Fort Smith, to which point steamers run during the seasons of high water in the winter and spring.

Supplies of all descriptions necessary for the overland journey may be procured at Fort Smith, or at Van Buren on the opposite side of the Arkansas.

Horses and cattle are cheap here. The road, on leaving Fort Smith, passes through the Choctaw and Chickasaw country for 180 miles, then crosses Red River by ferryboat at Preston, and runs through the border settlements of northern Texas for 150 miles, within which distances supplies may be procured at moderate prices.

This road is accessible to persons desiring to make the entire journey with their own transportation from Tennessee or Mississippi, by crossing the Mississippi River at Memphis or Helena, passing Little Rock, and thence through Washington County, intersecting the road at Preston. It may also be reached by taking steamers up Red River to Shreveport or Jefferson, from either of which places there are roads running through a populated country, and intersecting the Fort Smith road near Preston.

This road also unites with the San Antonio road at El Paso, and from that point they pass together over the mountains to Fort Yuma and to San Francisco in California.

Another road leaves Fort Smith and runs up the south side of the Canadian River to Santa Fé and Albuquerque in New Mexico.

This route is set down upon most of the maps of the present day as having been discovered and explored by various persons, but my own name seems to have been carefully excluded from the list. Whether this omission has been intentional or not, I leave for the authors to determine. I shall merely remark that I had the command and entire direction of an expedition which in 1849 discovered, explored, located, and marked out this identical wagon road from Fort Smith, Arkansas, to Santa Fé, New Mexico, and that this road, for the greater portion of the distance, is the same that has been since recommended for a Pacific railway.

This road, near Albuquerque, unites with Captain Whipple's and Lieutenant Beall's roads to California.

Another road, which takes its departure from Fort Smith and passes through the Cherokee country, is called the "Cherokee Trail." It crosses Grand River at Fort Gibson, and runs a little north of west to the Verdigris River, thence up the valley of this stream on the north side for 80 miles, when it crosses the river, and, taking a northwest course, strikes the Arkansas River near old Fort Mann, on the Santa Fé trace; thence it passes near the base of Pike's Peak, and follows down Cherry Creek from its source to its confluence with the South Platte, and from thence over the mountains into Utah, and on to California via Fort Bridger and Salt Lake City.

For persons who desire to go from the Southern States to the gold diggings in the vicinity of Cherry Creek, this route is shorter by some 300 miles than that from Fort Smith via Fort Leavenworth. It is said to be an excellent road, and well supplied with the requisites for encamping. It has been traveled by large parties of California emigrants for several years, and is well tracked and defined.

The grass upon all the roads leaving Fort Smith is sufficiently advanced to afford sustenance to animals by the first of April, and from this time until winter sets in it is abundant. The next route on the north leaves the Missouri River at Westport, Leavenworth City, Atcheson, or from other towns above, between either of which points and St. Louis steamers ply during the entire summer season.

The necessary outfit of supplies can always be procured at any of the starting points on the Missouri River at moderate rates.

This is the great emigrant route from Missouri to California and Oregon, over which so many thousands have traveled within the past few years. The track is broad, well worn, and cannot be mistaken. It has received the major part of the Mormon emigration, and was traversed by the army in its march to Utah in 1857.

At the point where this road crosses the South Platte River, Lieutenant Bryan's road branches off to the left, leading through Bridger's Pass, and thence to Fort Bridger. The Fort Kearney route to the gold region near Pike's Peak also leaves the emigrant road at this place and runs up the South Platte.

From Fort Bridger there are two roads that may be traveled with wagons in the direction of California; one passing Salt Lake City, and the other running down Bear River to Soda Springs, intersecting the Salt Lake City road at the City of Rocks. Near Soda Springs the Oregon road turns to the right, passing Fort Hall, and thence down Snake River to Fort Wallah-Wallah. Unless travelers have business in Salt Lake Valley, I would advise them to take the Bear River route, as it is much shorter, and better in every respect. The road, on leaving the Missouri River, passes for 150 miles through a settled country where grain can be purchased cheap, and there are several stores in this section where most of the articles required by travelers can be obtained.

Many persons who have had much experience in prairie traveling prefer leaving the Missouri River in March or April, and feeding grain to their animals until the new grass appears. The roads become muddy and heavy after the spring rains set in, and by starting out early the worst part of the road will be passed over before the ground becomes wet and soft. This plan, however, should never be attempted unless the animals are well supplied with grain, and kept in good condition. They will eat the old grass in the spring, but it does not, in this climate, as in Utah and New Mexico, afford them sufficient sustenance.

The grass, after the 1st of May, is good and abundant upon this road as far as the South Pass, from whence there is a section of about 50 miles where it is scarce; there is also a scarcity upon the desert beyond the sink of the Humboldt. As large numbers of cattle pass over the road annually, they soon consume all the grass in these barren localities, and such as pass late in the season are likely to suffer greatly, and oftentimes perish from starvation. When I came over the road in August, 1858, I seldom found myself out of sight of dead cattle for 500 miles along the road, and this was an unusually favorable year for grass, and before the main body of animals had passed for that season.

Upon the head of the Sweetwater River, and west of the South Pass, alkaline springs are met with, which are exceedingly poisonous to cattle and horses. They can readily be detected by the yellowish-red color of the grass growing around them. Animals should never be allowed to graze near them or to drink the water.

ORGANIZATION OF COMPANIES.

After a particular route has been selected to make the journey across the plains, and the requisite number have arrived at the eastern terminus, their first business should be to organize themselves into a company and elect a commander. The company should be of sufficient magnitude to herd and guard animals, and for protection against Indians.

From 50 to 70 men, properly armed and equipped, will be enough for these purposes, and any greater number only makes the movements of the party more cumbersome and tardy.

In the selection of a captain, good judgment, integrity of purpose, and practical experience are the essential requisites, and these are indispensable to the harmony and consolidation of the association. His duty should be to direct the order of march, the time of starting and halting, to select the camps, detail and give orders to guards, and, indeed, to control and superintend all the movements of the company.

An obligation should then be drawn up and signed by all the members of the association, wherein each one should bind himself to abide in all cases by the orders and decisions of the captain, and to aid him by every means in his power in the execution of his duties; and they should also obligate themselves to aid each other, so as to make the individual interest of each member the common concern of the whole company. To ensure this, a fund should be raised for the purchase of extra animals to supply the places of those which may give out or die on the road; and if the wagon or team of a particular member should fail and have to be abandoned, the company should obligate themselves to transport his luggage, and the captain should see that he has his share of transportation equal with any other member. Thus it will be made the interest of every member of the company to watch over and protect the property of others as well as his own.

In case of failure on the part of anyone to comply with the obligations imposed by the articles of agreement after they have been duly executed, the company should of course have the power to punish the delinquent member, and, if necessary, to exclude him from all the benefits of the association.

On such a journey as this, there is much to interest and amuse one who is fond of picturesque scenery, and of wildlife in its most primitive aspect, yet no one should attempt it without anticipating many rough knocks and much hard labor; every man must expect to do his share of duty faithfully and without a murmur.

On long and arduous expeditions men are apt to become irritable and ill-natured, and oftentimes fancy they have more labor imposed upon them than their comrades, and that the person who directs the march is partial toward his favorites, etc. That man who exercises the greatest forbearance under such circumstances, who is cheerful, slow to take up quarrels, and endeavors to reconcile difficulties among his companions, is deserving of all praise, and will, without doubt, contribute largely to the success and comfort of an expedition.

The advantages of an association such as I have mentioned are manifestly numerous. The animals can be herded together and guarded by the different members of the company in rotation, thereby securing to all the opportunities of sleep and rest. Besides, this is the only way to resist depredations of the Indians, and to prevent their stampeding and driving off animals; and much more efficiency is secured in every respect, especially in crossing streams, repairing roads, etc., etc.

Unless a systematic organization be adopted, it is impossible for a party of any magnitude to travel in company for any great length of time, and for all the members to agree upon the same arrangements in marching, camping, etc. I have several times observed, where this has been attempted, that discords and dissensions sooner or later arose which invariably resulted in breaking up and separating the company.

When a captain has once been chosen, he should be sustained in all his decisions unless he commit some manifest outrage, when a majority of the company can always remove him, and put a more competent man in his place. Sometimes men may be selected who, upon trial, do not come up to the anticipations of those who have placed them in power, and other men will exhibit, during the course of the march, more capacity. Under these circumstances it will not be unwise to make a change, the first election having been distinctly provisional.

WAGONS AND TEAMS.

A company having been organized, its first interest is to procure a proper outfit of transportation and supplies for the contemplated journey.

Wagons should be of the simplest possible construction—strong, light, and made of well-seasoned timber, especially the wheels, as the atmosphere, in the elevated and arid region over which they have to pass, is so exceedingly dry during the summer months that, unless the woodwork is thoroughly seasoned, they will require constant repairs to prevent them from falling to pieces.

Wheels made of the bois-d'arc, or Osage orange-wood, are the best for the plains, as they shrink but little, and seldom want repairing. As, however, this wood is not easily procured in the Northern States, white oak answers a very good purpose if well seasoned.

Spring wagons made in Concord, New Hampshire, are used to transport passengers and the mails upon some of the routes across the plains, and they are said, by those who have used them, to be much superior to any others. They are made of the close-grained oak that grows in a high northern latitude, and well seasoned.

The pole of the wagon should have a joint where it enters the hounds, to prevent the weight from coming upon it and breaking the hounds in passing short and abrupt holes in the road.

The perch or coupling pole should be shifting or movable, as, in the event of the loss of a wheel, an axle, or other accident rendering it necessary to abandon the wagon, a temporary cart may be constructed out of the remaining portion. The tires should be examined just before commencing the journey, and, if not perfectly snug, reset.

One of the chief causes of accidents to carriages upon the plains arises from the nuts coming off from the numerous bolts that secure the running gearing. To prevent this, the ends of all the bolts should be riveted; it is seldom necessary to take them off, and when this is required the ends of the bolts may easily be filed away.

Wagons with six mules should never, on a long journey over the prairies, be loaded with over 2000 pounds, unless grain is transported, when an additional thousand pounds may be taken, provided it is fed out daily to the team. When grass constitutes the only forage, 2000 pounds is deemed a sufficient load. I regard our government wagons as unnecessarily heavy for six mules. There is sufficient material in them to sustain a burden of 4000 pounds, but they are seldom loaded with more than half that weight. Every wagon should be furnished with substantial bows and double osnaburg covers, to protect its contents from the sun and weather.

There has been much discussion regarding the relative merits of mules and oxen for prairie traveling, and the question is yet far from being settled. Upon good firm roads, in a populated country, where grain can be procured, I should unquestionably give the preference to mules, as they travel faster, and endure the heat of summer much better than oxen; and if the journey be not over 1000 miles, and the grass abundant, even without grain, I think mules would be preferable. But when the march is to extend 1500 or 2000 miles, or over a rough, sandy or muddy road, I believe young oxen will endure better than mules; they will, if properly managed, keep in better condition, and perform the journey in an equally brief space of time. Besides, they are much more economical, a team of six mules costing six hundred dollars, while an eight-ox team only costs upon the frontier about two hundred dollars. Oxen are much less liable to be stampeded and driven off by Indians; and can be pursued and overtaken by horsemen; and, finally, they can, if necessary, be used for beef.

In Africa oxen are used as saddle animals, and it is said that they perform good service in this way. This will probably be regarded by our people as a very undignified and singular method of locomotion, but, in the absence of any other means of transportation upon a long journey, a saddle-ox might be found serviceable.

Andersson, in his work on Southwestern Africa, says: "A short strong stick, of peculiar shape, is forced through the cartilage of the nose of the ox, and to either end of this stick is attached (in bridle fashion) a tough leathern thong. From the extreme tenderness of the nose he is now more easily managed.

"Hans presented me with an ox called 'Spring,' which I afterward rode upward of two thousand miles. On the day of our departure he mounted us all on oxen, and a curious sight it was to see some of the men take their seats who had never before ridden on ox-back. It is impossible to guide an ox as one would guide a horse, for in the attempt to do so you would instantly jerk the stick out of his nose, which at once deprives you of every control over the beast; but by pulling *both* sides of the bridle at the same time, and toward the side you wish him to take, he is easily managed.* Your seat is not less awkward and difficult; for the skin of the ox, unlike that of the horse, is loose, and, notwithstanding your saddle may be tightly girthed, you keep rocking to and fro like a child in a cradle. A few days, however, enables a person to acquire a certain steadiness, and long habit will do the rest.

"Ox traveling, when once a man becomes accustomed to it, is not so disagreeable as might be expected, particularly if one succeeds in obtaining a tractable animal. On emergencies, an ox can be made to proceed at a tolerable quick pace; for, though his walk is only about three miles an hour at an average, he may be made to perform double that distance in the same time. Mr. Galton once accomplished 24 miles in four hours, and that, too, through heavy sand!"

Cows will be found very useful upon long journeys when the rate of travel is slow, as they furnish milk, and in emergencies they may be worked in wagons. I once saw a small cow yoked beside a large

* A ring instead of the stick put through the cartilage of the nose would obviate this difficulty.—AUTHOR

ox, and driven about six hundred miles attached to a loaded wagon, and she performed her part equally well with the ox. It has been by no means an unusual thing for emigrant travelers to work cows in their teams.

The inhabitants of Pembina, on Red River, work a single ox harnessed in shafts like a horse, and they transport a thousand pounds in a rude cart made entirely of wood, without a particle of iron. One man drives and takes the entire charge of eight or ten of these teams upon long journeys. This is certainly a very economical method of transportation.

STORES AND PROVISIONS.

Supplies for a march should be put up in the most secure, compact, and portable shape.

Bacon should be packed in strong sacks of a hundred pounds to each; or, in very hot climates, put in boxes and surrounded with bran, which in a great measure prevents the fat from melting away.

If pork be used, in order to avoid transporting about forty percent of useless weight, it should be taken out of the barrels and packed like the bacon; then so placed in the bottom of the wagons as to keep it cool. The pork, if well cured, will keep several months in this way, but bacon is preferable.

Flour should be packed in stout double canvas sacks well sewed, a hundred pounds in each sack.

Butter may be preserved by boiling it thoroughly, and skimming off the scum as it rises to the top until it is quite clear like oil. It is then placed in tin canisters and soldered up. This mode of preserving butter has been adopted in the hot climate of southern Texas, and it is found to keep sweet for a great length of time, and its flavor is but little impaired by the process.

Sugar may be well secured in India rubber or gutta-percha sacks, or so placed in the wagon as not to risk getting wet.

Desiccated or dried vegetables are almost equal to the fresh, and are put up in such a compact and portable form as easily to be transported over the plains. They have been extensively used in the Crimean war, and by our own army in Utah, and have been very generally approved. They are prepared by cutting the fresh vegetables into thin slices and subjecting them to a very powerful press, which removes the juice and leaves a solid cake, which, after having been thoroughly dried in an oven, becomes almost as hard as a rock. A small piece of this, about half the size of a man's hand, when boiled, swells up so as to fill a vegetable dish, and is sufficient for four men. It is believed that the antiscorbutic properties of vegetables are not impaired by desiccation, and they will keep for years if not exposed to dampness. Canned vegetables are very good for campaigning, but are not so portable as when put up in the other form. The desiccated vegetables used in our army have been prepared by Chollet and Co., 46 Rue Richer, Paris. There is an agency for them in New York. I regard these compressed vegetables as the best preparation for prairie traveling that has yet been discovered. A single ration weighs, before being boiled, only an ounce, and a cubic yard contains 16,000 rations. In making up their outfit for the plains, men are very prone to overload their teams with a great variety of useless articles. It is a good rule to carry nothing more than is absolutely necessary for use upon the journey. One cannot expect, with the limited allowance of transportation that emigrants usually have, to indulge in luxuries upon such expeditions, and articles for use in California can be purchased there at less cost than that of overland transport.

The allowance of provisions for men in marching should be much greater than when they take no exercise. The army ration I have always found insufficient for soldiers who perform hard service, yet it is ample for them when in quarters.

The following table shows the amount of subsistence consumed per day by each man of Dr. Rae's party, in his spring journey to the Arctic regions of North America in 1854:

Pemmican	1.25	lbs.
Biscuit	0.25	"
Edward's preserved potatoes	0.10	"
Flour	0.33	"
Tea	0.03	"
Sugar	0.14	"
Grease or alcohol, for cooking	0.25	"
	2.35	lbs.

This allowance of a little over two pounds of the most nutritious food was found barely sufficient to subsist the men in that cold climate.

The pemmican, which constitutes almost the entire diet of the Fur Company's men in the Northwest, is prepared as follows: The buffalo meat is cut into thin flakes, and hung up to dry in the sun or before a slow fire; it is then pounded between two stones and reduced to a powder; this powder is placed in a bag of the animal's hide, with the hair on the outside; melted grease is then poured into it, and the bag sewn up. It can be eaten raw, and many prefer it so. Mixed with a little flour and boiled, it is a very wholesome and exceedingly nutritious food, and will keep fresh for a long time.

I would advise all persons who travel for any considerable time through a country where they can procure no vegetables to carry with them some antiscorbutics, and if they cannot transport desiccated or canned vegetables, citric acid answers a good purpose, and is very portable. When mixed with sugar and water, with a few drops of the essence of lemon, it is difficult to distinguish it from lemonade. Wild onions are excellent as antiscorbutics; also wild grapes and greens. An infusion of hemlock leaves is also said to be an antidote to scurvy.

The most portable and simple preparation of subsistence that I know of, and which is used extensively by the Mexicans and Indians, is called "cold flour." It is made by parching corn, and pounding it in a mortar to the consistency of coarse meal; a little sugar and cinnamon added makes it quite palatable. When the traveler becomes hungry or thirsty, a little of the flour is mixed with water and drunk. It is an excellent article for a traveler who desires to go the greatest length of time upon the smallest amount of transportation. It is said that half a bushel is sufficient to subsist a man thirty days.

Persons undergoing severe labor, and driven to great extremities for food, will derive sustenance from various sources that would never occur to them under ordinary circumstances. In passing over the Rocky Mountains during the winter of 1857–8, our supplies of provisions were entirely consumed eighteen days before reaching the first settlements in New Mexico, and we were obliged to resort to a variety of expedients to supply the deficiency. Our poor mules were fast failing and dropping down from exhaustion in the deep snows, and our only dependence for the means of sustaining life was upon these starved animals as they became unserviceable and could go no farther. We had no salt, sugar, coffee, or tobacco, which, at a time when men are performing the severest labor that the human system is capable of enduring, was a great privation. In this destitute condition we found a substitute for tobacco in the bark of the red willow, which grows upon many of the mountain streams in that vicinity. The outer bark is first removed with a knife, after which the inner bark is scraped up into ridges around the sticks, and held in the fire until it is thoroughly roasted, when it is taken off the stick, pulverized in the hand, and is ready for smoking. It has the narcotic properties of the tobacco, and is quite agreeable to the taste and smell. The sumach leaf is also used by the Indians in the same way, and has a similar taste to the willow bark. A decoction of the dried wild or horse mint, which we found abundant under the snow, was quite palatable, and answered instead of coffee. It dries up in that climate, but does not lose its flavor. We suffered greatly for the want of salt; but, by burning the outside of our mule steaks, and sprinkling a little gunpowder upon them, it did not require a very extensive stretch of the imagination to fancy the presence of both salt and pepper. We tried the meat of horse, colt, and mules, all of which were in a starved condition, and of course not very tender, juicy, or nutritious. We consumed the enormous amount of from five to six pounds of this meat per man daily, but continued to grow weak and thin, until, at the expiration of twelve days, we were able to perform but little labor, and were continually craving for fat meat.

The allowance of provisions for each grown person, to make the journey from the Missouri River to California, should suffice for 110 days. The following is deemed requisite, viz.: 150 lbs. of flour, or its equivalent in hard bread; 25 lbs. of bacon or pork, and enough fresh beef to be driven on the hoof to make up the meat component of the ration; 15 lbs. of coffee, and 25 lbs. of sugar; also a quantity of saleratus or yeast powders for making bread, and salt and pepper.

These are the chief articles of subsistence necessary for the trip, and they should be used with economy, reserving a good portion for the western half of the journey. Heretofore many of the California emigrants have improvidently exhausted their stocks of provisions before reaching their journey's end, and have, in many cases, been obliged to pay the most exorbitant prices in making up the deficiency.

It is true that if persons choose to pass through Salt Lake City, and the Mormons happen to be in an amiable mood, supplies may sometimes be procured from them; but those who have visited them well know how little reliance is to be placed upon their hospitality or spirit of accommodation.

I once traveled with a party of New Yorkers en route for California. They were perfectly ignorant of everything relating to this kind of campaigning, and had overloaded their wagons with almost everything except the very articles most important and necessary; the consequence was, that they exhausted their teams, and were obliged to throw away the greater part of their loading. They soon learned that Champagne, East India sweetmeats, olives, etc., etc., were not the most useful articles for a prairie tour.

CLOTHING.

A suitable dress for prairie traveling is of great import to health and comfort. Cotton or linen fabrics do not sufficiently protect the body against the direct rays of the sun at midday, nor against rains or sudden changes of temperature. Wool, being a non-conductor, is the best material for this mode of locomotion, and should always be adopted for the plains. The coat should be short and stout, the shirt of red or blue flannel, such as can be found in almost all the shops on the frontier: this, in warm weather, answers for an outside garment. The pants should be of thick and soft woolen material, and it is well to have them reenforced on the inside, where they come in contact with the saddle, with soft buckskin, which makes them more durable and comfortable.

Woolen socks and stout boots, coming up well at the knees, and made large, so as to admit the pants, will be found the best for horsemen, and they guard against rattlesnake bites.

In traveling through deep snow during very cold weather in winter, moccasins are preferable to boots or shoes, as being more pliable, and allowing a freer circulation of the blood. In crossing the Rocky Mountains in the winter, the weather being intensely cold, I wore two pairs of woolen socks, and a square piece of thick blanket sufficient to cover the feet and ankles, over which were drawn a pair of thick buckskin moccasins, and the whole enveloped in a pair of buffalo-skin boots with the hair inside, made open in the front and tied with buckskin strings. At the same time I wore a pair of elkskin pants, which most effectually prevented the air from penetrating to the skin, and made an excellent defense against brush and thorns.

My men, who were dressed in the regulation clothing, wore out their pants and shoes before we reached the summit of the mountains, and many of them had their feet badly frozen in consequence. They mended their shoes with pieces of leather cut from the saddle skirts as long as they lasted, and, when this material was gone, they covered the entire shoe with green beeve or mule hide, drawn together and sewed upon the top, with the hair inside, which protected the upper as well as the sole leather. The sewing was done with an awl and buckskin strings. These simple expedients contributed greatly to the comfort of the party; and, indeed, I am by no means sure that they did not, in our straitened condition, without the transportation necessary for carrying disabled men, save the lives of some of them. Without the awl and buckskins we should have been unable to have repaired the shoes. They should never be forgotten in making up the outfit for a prairie expedition.

We also experienced great inconvenience and pain by the reflection of the sun's rays from the snow upon our eyes, and some of the party became nearly snow-blind. Green or blue glasses, enclosed in a wire network, are an effectual protection to the eyes; but, in the absence of these, the skin around the eyes and upon the nose should be blackened with wet powder or charcoal, which will afford great relief.

In the summer season shoes are much better for footmen than boots, as they are lighter, and do not cramp the ankles; the soles should be broad, so as to allow a square, firm tread, without distorting or pinching the feet.

The following list of articles is deemed a sufficient outfit for one man upon a three months' expedition, viz.:

2 blue or red flannel overshirts, open in front with buttons.
2 woolen undershirts.
2 pairs thick cotton drawers.
4 pairs woolen socks.
2 pairs cotton socks.
4 colored silk handkerchiefs.
2 pairs stout shoes, for footmen.
1 pair boots, for horsemen.
1 pair shoes, for horsemen.
3 towels.
1 gutta percha poncho.
1 broad-brimmed hat of soft felt
1 comb and brush
2 tooth-brushes.
1 pound Castile soap.
3 pounds bar soap for washing clothes.
1 belt-knife and small whetstone.
Stout linen thread, large needles, a bit of beeswax, a few buttons, paper of pins, and a thimble, all contained in a small buckskin or stout cloth bag.

The foregoing articles, with the coat and overcoat, complete the wardrobe.

CAMP EQUIPAGE.

The bedding for each person should consist of two blankets, a comforter, and a pillow, and a gutta percha or painted canvas cloth to spread beneath the bed upon the ground, and to contain it when rolled up for transportation.

Every mess of six or eight persons will require a wrought-iron camp kettle, large enough for boiling meat and making soup; a coffeepot and cups of heavy tin, with the handles riveted on; tin plates, frying and bake pans of wrought iron, the latter for baking bread and roasting coffee. Also a mess pan of heavy tin or wrought iron for mixing bread and other culinary purposes; knives, forks, and spoons; an extra camp kettle; tin or gutta-percha bucket for water—wood, being liable to shrink and fall to pieces, is not deemed suitable; an axe, hatchet, and spade will also be needed, with a mallet for driving picket pins. Matches should be carried in bottles and corked tight, so as to exclude the moisture.

A little blue mass, quinine, opium, and some cathartic medicine, put up in doses for adults, will suffice for the medicine chest.

Each ox wagon should be provided with a covered tar-bucket, filled with a mixture of tar or resin and grease, two bows extra, six S's, and six open links for repairing chains. Every set of six wagons should have a tongue, coupling pole, kingbolt, and pair of hounds extra.

Every set of six mule wagons should be furnished with five pairs of hames, two double trees, four whipple trees, and two pairs of lead bars extra.

Two lariats will be needed for every horse and mule, as one generally wears out before reaching the end of a long journey. They will be found useful in crossing deep streams, and in letting wagons down steep hills and mountains; also in repairing broken wagons. Lariats made of hemp are the best.

One of the most indispensable articles to the outfit of the prairie traveler is buckskin. For repairing harness, saddles, bridles, and numerous other purposes of daily necessity, the awl and buckskin will be found in constant requisition.

ARMS.

Every man who goes into the Indian country should be armed with a rifle and revolver, and he should never, either in camp or out of it, lose sight of them. When not on the march, they should be placed in such a position that they can be seized at an instant's warning; and when moving about outside the camp, the revolver should invariably be worn in the belt, as the person does not know at what moment he may have use for it.

A great diversity of opinion obtains regarding the kind of rifle that is the most efficient and best adapted to Indian warfare, and the question is perhaps as yet very far from being settled to the satisfaction of all. A large majority of men prefer the breech-loading arm, but there are those who still adhere tenaciously to the old-fashioned muzzle-loading rifle as preferable to any of the modern inventions. Among these may be mentioned the border hunters and mountaineers, who cannot be persuaded to use any other than the Hawkins rifle, for the reason that they know nothing about the merits of any others. My own experience has forced me to the conclusion that the breech-loading arm possesses great advantages over the muzzle-loading, for the reason that it can be charged and fired with much greater rapidity.

Colt's revolving pistol is very generally admitted, both in Europe and America, to be the most efficient arm of its kind known at the present day. As the same principles are involved in the fabrication of his breech-loading rifle as are found in the pistol, the conviction to me is irresistible that, if one arm is worthy of consideration, the other is equally so. For my own part, I look upon Colt's new patent rifle as a most excellent arm for border service. It gives six shots in more rapid succession than any other rifle I know of, and these, if properly expended, are oftentimes sufficient to decide a contest; moreover, it is the most reliable and certain weapon to fire that I have ever used, and I cannot resist the force of my conviction that, if I were alone upon the prairies, and expected an attack from a body of Indians, I am not acquainted with any arm I would as soon have in my hands as this.

The army and navy revolvers have both been used in our army, but the officers are not united in opinion in regard to their relative merits. I prefer the large army size, for reasons which will be given hereafter.

CHAPTER II.

Marching. —Treatment of Animals. —Water. —Different methods of finding and purifying it.—Journadas.—Methods of crossing them.—Advance and Rear Guards.--Selection of Camp.—Sanitary Considerations.—Dr. Jackson's Report.—Picket Guards.—Stampedes.—How to prevent them. Corraling Wagons.

MARCHING.

THE SUCCESS of a long expedition through an unpopulated country depends mainly on the care taken of the animals, and the manner in which they are driven, herded, and guarded. If they are broken down or lost, everything must be sacrificed, and the party becomes perfectly helpless.

The great error into which inexperienced travelers are liable to fall, and which probably occasions more suffering and disaster than almost anything else, lies in overworking their cattle at the commencement of the journey. To obviate this, short and easy drives should be made until the teams become habituated to their work, and gradually inured to this particular method of traveling. If animals are overloaded and overworked when they first start out into the prairies, especially if they have recently been taken from grain, they soon fall away, and give out before reaching the end of the journey.

Grass and water are abundant and good upon the eastern portions of all the different overland routes; animals should not, therefore, with proper care, fall away in the least before reaching the mountains, as west of them are long stretches where grass and water are scarce, and it requires the full amount of strength and vigor of animals in good condition to endure the fatigues and hard labor attendant upon the passage of these deserts. Drivers should be closely watched, and never, unless absolutely necessary, permitted to beat their animals, or to force them out of a walk, as this will soon break down the best teams. Those teamsters who make the least use of the whip invariably keep their animals in the best condition. Unless the drivers are checked at the outset, they are very apt to fall into the habit of flogging their teams. It is not only wholly unnecessary but cruel, and should never be tolerated.

In traveling with ox teams in the summer season, great benefit will be derived from making early marches; starting with the dawn, and making a "nooning" during the heat of the day, as oxen suffer much from the heat of the sun in midsummer. These noon halts should, if possible, be so arranged as to be near grass and water, where the animals can improve their time in grazing. When it gets cool they may be hitched to the wagons again, and the journey continued in the afternoon. Sixteen or eighteen miles a day may thus be made without injury to the beasts, and longer drives can never be expedient, unless in order to reach grass or water. When the requisites for encamping cannot be found at the desired intervals, it is better for the animals to make a very long drive than to encamp without water or grass. The noon halt in such cases may be made without water, and the evening drive lengthened.

WATER.

The scarcity of water upon some of the routes across the plains occasionally exposes the traveler to intense suffering, and renders it a matter of much importance for him to learn the best methods of guarding against the disasters liable to occur to men and animals in the absence of this most necessary element.

In mountainous districts water can generally be found either in springs, the dry beds of streams, or in holes in the rocks, where they are sheltered from rapid evaporation. For example, in the Hueco tanks, thirty miles east of El Paso, New Mexico, upon the Fort Smith road, where there is an immense reservoir in a cave, water can always be found. This reservoir receives the drainage of a mountain.

During a season of the year when there are occasional showers, water will generally be found in low places where there is a substratum of clay, but after the dry season has set in these pools evaporate, and it is necessary to dig wells. The lowest spots should be selected for this purpose when the grass is green and the surface earth moist.

In searching for water along the dry sandy beds of streams, it is well to try the earth with a stick or ramrod, and if this indicates moisture, water will generally be obtained by excavation. Streams often sink in light and porous sand, and sometimes make their appearance again lower down, where the bed is more tenacious; but it is a rule with prairie travelers, in searching for water in a sandy country, to ascend the streams, and the nearer their sources are approached the more water will be found in a dry season.

Where it becomes necessary to sink a well in a stream the bed of which is quicksand, a flour barrel, perforated with small holes, should be used as a curb, to prevent the sand from caving in. The barrel must be forced down as the sand is removed; and when, as is often the case, there is an undercurrent through the sand, the well will be continually filled with water.

There are many indications of water known to old campaigners, although none of them are absolutely infallible. The most certain of them are deep green cottonwood or willow trees growing in depressed localities; also flags, water rushes, tall green grass, etc.

The fresh tracks and trails of animals converging toward a common center, and the flight of birds and waterfowl toward the same points, will also lead to water. In a section frequented by deer or mustangs, it may be certain that water is not far distant, as these animals drink daily, and they will not remain long in a locality after the water has dried up. Deer generally go to water during the middle of the day, but birds toward evening.

A supply of drinking water may be obtained during a shower from the drippings of a tent, or by suspending a cloth or blanket by the four corners and hanging a small weight to the center, so as to allow all the rain to run toward one point, from whence it drops into a vessel beneath. India rubber, gutta-percha, or painted canvas cloths answer a very good purpose for catching water during a rain, but they should be previously well washed, to prevent them from imparting a bad taste.

When there are heavy dews water may be collected by spreading out a blanket with a stick attached to one end, tying a rope to it, dragging it over the grass, and wringing out the water as it accumulates. In some parts of Australia this method is practiced.

In traversing the country upon the headwaters of Red River during the summer of 1852, we suffered most severely from thirst, having nothing but the acrid and bitter waters from the river, which, issuing from a gypsum formation, was highly charged with salts, and, when taken into the stomach, did not quench thirst in the slightest degree, but, on the contrary, produced a most painful and burning sensation, accompanied with diarrhea. During the four days that we were compelled to drink this water the thermometer rose to 104° in the shade, and the only relief we found was from bathing in the river.

The use of water is a matter of habit, very much within our control, as by practice we may discipline ourselves so as to require but a small amount. Some persons, for example, who place no restraint upon their appetites, will, if they can get it, drink water twenty times a day, while others will not perhaps drink more than once or twice during the same time. I have found a very effectual preventive to thirst by drinking a large quantity of water before breakfast, and, on feeling thirsty on the march, chewing a small green twig or leaf.

Water taken from stagnant pools, charged with putrid vegetable matter and animalcula, would be very likely to generate fevers and dysenteries if taken into the stomach without purification. It should therefore be thoroughly boiled, and all the scum removed from the surface as it rises; this clarifies it, and by mixing powdered charcoal with it the disinfecting process is perfected. Water may also be purified by placing a piece of alum in the end of a stick that has been split, and stirring it around in a bucket of water. Charcoal and the leaves of the prickly pear are also used for the same purpose. I have recently seen a compact and portable filter, made of charcoal, which clarifies the water very effectually, and draws it off on the siphon principle. It can be obtained at 85 West Street, New York, for one dollar and a half. Water may be partially filtered in a muddy pond by taking a barrel and boring the lower half full of holes, then filling it up with grass or moss above the upper holes, after which it is placed in the pond with the top above the surface. The water filters through the grass or moss, and rises in the barrel to a level with the pond. Travelers frequently drink muddy water by placing a cloth or handkerchief over the mouth of a cup to catch the larger particles of dirt and animalcula.

Water may be cooled so as to be quite palatable by wrapping cloths around the vessels containing it, wetting them, and hanging them in the air, where a rapid evaporation will be produced. Some of the frontiersmen use a leathern sack for carrying water: this is porous, and allows the necessary evaporation without wetting.

The Arabs also use a leathern bottle, which they call *zemsemiyah.* When they are en route they hang it on the shady side of a camel, where the evaporation keeps the water continually cool.

No expedition should ever set out into the plains without being supplied with the means for carrying water, especially in an unknown region. If wooden kegs are used they must frequently be looked after, and soaked, in order that they may not shrink and fall to pieces. Men, in marching in a hot climate, throw off a great amount of perspiration from the skin, and require a corresponding quantity of water to supply the deficiency, and unless they get this they suffer greatly. When a party makes an expedition into a desert section, where there is a probability of finding no water, and intend to return over the same track, it is well to carry water as far as convenient, and bury it in the ground for use on the return trip.

"Captain Sturt, when he explored Australia, took a tank in his cart, which burst, and, besides that, he carried casks of water. By these he was enabled to face a desert country with a success which no traveler had ever attained to. For instance, when returning homeward, the water was found to be drying up from the country on all sides of him. He was at a pool, and the next stage was 118 miles, at the end of which it was doubtful if there remained any water. It was necessary to send to reconnoiter, and to furnish the messenger with means of returning should the pool be found dry. He killed a bullock, skinned it, and, filling the skin with water (which held 150 gallons), sent it by an ox dray 30 miles, with orders to bury it and to return. Shortly after he dispatched a light one-horse cart, carrying 36 gallons of water; the horse and man were to drink at the hide and go on. Thus they had 36 gallons to supply them for a journey of 176 miles, or six days at 30 miles a day, at the close of which they would return to the ox hide—sleeping, in fact, five nights on 36 gallons of water. This a hardy, well-driven horse could do, even in the hottest climate."*

* F. Galton's *Art of Travel*, pp. 17 and 18.

JOURNADAS

In some localities 50 or 60 miles, and even greater distances, are frequently traversed without water; these long stretches are called by the Mexicans *journadas,* or day's journeys. There is one in New Mexico called *Journada del Muerto,* which is 78½ miles in length, where, in a dry season, there is not a drop of water; yet, with proper care, this drive can be made with ox or mule teams, and without loss or injury to the animals.

On arriving at the last camping ground before entering upon the journada, all the animals should be as well rested and refreshed as possible. To ensure this, they must be turned out upon the best grass that can be found, and allowed to eat and drink as much as they desire during the entire halt. Should the weather be very warm, and the teams composed of oxen, the march should not be resumed until it begins to cool in the afternoon. They should be carefully watered just previous to being hitched up and started out upon the journada, the water kegs having been previously filled. The drive is then commenced, and continued during the entire night, with 10 or 15 minutes rest every two hours. About daylight a halt should be made, and the animals immediately turned out to graze for two hours, during which time, especially if there is dew upon the grass, they will have become considerably refreshed, and may be put to the wagons again and driven until the heat becomes oppressive toward noon, when they are again turned out upon a spot where the grass is good, and, if possible, where there are shade trees. About four o'clock P.M. they are again started, and the march continued into the night, and as long as they can be driven without suffering. If, however, there should be dew, which is seldom the case on the plains, it would be well to turn out the animals several times during the second night, and by morning, if they are in good condition, the journada of 70 or 80 miles will have been passed without any great amount of suffering. I am supposing, in this case, that the road is firm and free from sand.

Many persons have been under the impression that animals, in traversing the plains, would perform better and keep in better condition by allowing them to graze in the morning before commencing the day's march, which involves the necessity of making late starts, and driving during the heat of the day. The same persons have been of the opinion that animals will graze only at particular hours; that the remainder of the day must be allowed them for rest and sleep, and that, unless these rules be observed, they would not thrive. This opinion is, however, erroneous, as animals will in a few days adapt themselves to any circumstances, so far as regards their hours of labor, rest, and refreshment. If they have been accustomed to work at particular periods of the day, and the order of things is suddenly reversed, the working hours changed into hours of rest, and vice versa, they may not do as well for a short time, but they will soon accustom themselves to the change, and eat and rest as well as before. By making early drives during the summer months the heat of the day is avoided, whereas, I repeat, if allowed to graze before starting, the march cannot commence until it grows warm, when animals, especially oxen, will suffer greatly from the heat of the sun, and will not do as well as when the other plan is pursued.

Oxen upon a long journey will sometimes wear down their hoofs and become lame. When this occurs, a thick piece of rawhide wrapped around the foot and tied firmly to the leg will obviate the difficulty, provided the weather is not wet; for if so, the shoe soon wears out. Mexican and Indian horses and mules will make long journeys without being shod, as their hoofs are tough and elastic, and wear away very gradually; they will, however, in time become very smooth, making it difficult for them to travel upon grass.

A train of wagons should always be kept closed upon a march; and if, as often happens, a particular wagon gets out of order and is obliged to halt, it should be turned out of the road, to let the others pass while the injury is being repaired. As soon as the broken wagon is in order, it should fall into the line wherever it happens to be. In the event of a wagon breaking down so as to require important repairs, men should be immediately dispatched with the necessary tools and materials, which should be placed in the train where they can readily be got at, and a guard should be left to escort the wagon to camp after having been repaired. If, however, the damage be so serious as to require any great length of time to repair it, the load should be transferred to other wagons, so that the team which is left behind will be able to travel rapidly and overtake the train.

If the broken wagon is a poor one, and there be abundance of better ones, the accident being such as to involve much delay for its repair, it may be wise to abandon it, taking from it such parts as may possibly be wanted in repairing other wagons.

ADVANCE AND REAR GUARDS.

A few men, well mounted, should constitute the advance and rear guards for each train of wagons passing through the Indian country. Their duty will be to keep a vigilant lookout in all directions, and to reconnoiter places where Indians would be likely to lie in ambush. Should hostile Indians be discovered, the fact should be at once reported to the commander, who (if he anticipates an attack) will rapidly form his wagons into a circle of "corral," with the animals toward the center, and the men on the inside, with their arms in readiness to repel an attack from without. If these arrangements be properly attended to, few parties of Indians will venture to make an attack, as they are well aware that some of their warriors might pay with their lives the forfeit of such indiscretion.

I know an instance where one resolute man, pursued for several days by a large party of Comanches on the Santa Fé trace, defended himself by dismounting and pointing his rifle at the foremost whenever they came near him, which always had the effect of turning them back. This was repeated so often that the Indians finally abandoned the pursuit, and left the traveler to pursue his journey without farther molestation. During all this time he did not discharge his rifle; had he done so he would doubtless have been killed.

SELECTION OF CAMPS.

The security of animals, and, indeed, the general safety of a party, in traveling through a country occupied by hostile Indians, depends greatly upon the judicious selection of camps. One of the most important considerations that should influence the choice of a locality is its capability for defense. If the camp be pitched beside a stream, a concave bend, where the water is deep, with a soft alluvial bed enclosed by high and abrupt banks, will be the most defensible, and all the more should the concavity form a peninsula. The advantages of such a position are obvious to a soldier's eye, as that part of the encampment enclosed by the stream is naturally secure, and leaves only one side to be defended. The concavity of the bend will enable the defending party to cross its fire in case of attack from the exposed side. The bend of the stream will also form an excellent corral in which to secure animals from a stampede, and thereby diminish the number of sentinels needful around the camp. In herding animals at night within the bend of a stream, a spot should be selected where no clumps of brush grow on the side where the animals are posted. If thickets of brush cannot be avoided, sentinels should be placed near them, to guard against Indians, who might take advantage of this cover to steal animals, or shoot them down with arrows, before their presence were known.

In camping away from streams, it is advisable to select a position in which one or more sides of the encampment shall rest upon the crest of an abrupt hill or bluff. The prairie Indians make their camps upon the summits of the hills, whence they can see in all directions, and thus avoid a surprise.

The line of tents should be pitched on that side of the camp most exposed to attack, and sentinels so posted that they may give alarm in time for the main body to rally and prepare for defense.

SANITARY CONSIDERATIONS.

When camping near rivers and lakes surrounded by large bodies of timber and a luxuriant vegetation, which produces a great amount of decomposition and consequent exhalations of malaria, it is important to ascertain what localities will be the least likely to generate disease, and to affect the sanitary condition of men occupying them.

This subject has been thoroughly examined by Dr. Robert Johnson, Inspector General of Hospitals in the English army of 1845; and, as his conclusions are deduced from enlarged experience and extended research, they should have great weight. I shall therefore make no apology for introducing here a few extracts from his interesting report touching upon this subject:

"It is consonant with the experience of military people, in all ages and in all countries, that camp diseases most abound near the muddy banks of large rivers, near swamps and ponds, and on grounds which have been recently stripped of their woods. The fact is precise, but it has been set aside to make way for an opinion. It was assumed, about half a century since, by a celebrated army physician, that camp diseases originated from causes of putrefaction, and that putrefaction is connected radically with a stagnant condition of the air.

"As streams of air usually proceed along rivers with more certainty and force than in other places, and as there is evidently a more certain movement of air, that is, more wind on open grounds than among woods and thickets, this sole consideration, without any regard to experience, influenced opinion, gave currency to the destructive maxim that the banks of rivers, open grounds, and exposed heights are the most eligible situations for the encampment of troops. They are the best ventilated; they must, if the theory be true, be the most healthy.

"The fact is the reverse; but, demonstrative as the fact may be, fashion has more influence than multiplied examples of fact experimentally proved. Encampments are still formed in the vicinity of swamps, or on grounds which are newly cleared of their woods, in obedience to theory, and contrary to fact.

"It is prudent, as now said, in *selecting ground for encampment*, to avoid the immediate vicinity of swamps and rivers. The air is there noxious; but, as its influence thence originating does not extend beyond a certain limit, it is a matter of some importance to ascertain to what distance it does extend; because, if circumstances do not permit that the encampment be removed out of its reach, prudence directs that remedies be applied to weaken the force of its pernicious impressions.

The remedies consist in the interposition of rising grounds, woods, or such other impediments as serve to break the current in its progress from the noxious source. It is an obvious fact, that the noxious cause, or the exhalation in which it is enveloped, ascends as it traverses the adjacent plain, and that its impression is augmented by the adventitious force with which it strikes upon the subject of its action.

"It is thus that a position of three hundred paces from the margin of a swamp, on a level with the swamp itself, or but moderately elevated, is less unhealthy than one at six hundred on the same line of direction on an exposed height. The cause here strikes fully in its ascent; and as the atmosphere has a more varied temperature, and the successions of the air are more irregular on the height than on the plain, the impression is more forcible, and the noxious effect more strongly marked. In accord with this principle, it is almost uniformly true, *cœteris paribus*, that diseases are more common, at least more violent, in broken, irregular, and hilly countries, where the temperature is liable to sudden changes, and where blasts descend with fury from the mountains, than in large and extensive inclined plains under the action of equal and gentle breezes only.

"From this fact it becomes an object of the first consideration, in selecting ground for encampment, to guard against the impression of strong winds on their own account, independently of their proceeding from swamps, rivers, and noxious soils.

"It is proved by experience, in armies as in civil life, that injury does not often result from simple wetting with rain when the person is fairly exposed in the open air, and habitually inured to the contingencies of weather. Irregular troops, which act in the advanced line of armies, and which have no other shelter from weather than a hedge or tree, rarely experience sickness—never, at least, the sickness which proceeds from contagion; hence it is inferred that the shelter of tents is not necessary for the preservation of health. Irregular troops, with contingent shelter only, are comparatively healthy, while sickness often rages with violence in the same scenæ, among those who have all the protection against the inclemencies of weather which can be furnished by canvas. The fact is verified by experience, and the cause of it is not of difficult explanation. When the earth is damp, the action of heat on its surface occasions the interior moisture to ascend. The heat of the bodies of a given number of men, confined within a tent of a given dimension, raises the temperature within the tent beyond the temperature of the common air outside the tent. The ascent of moisture is thus encouraged, generally by a change of temperature in the tent, and more particularly by the immediate or near contact of the heated bodies of the men with the surface of the earth. Moisture, as exhaled from the earth, is considered by observers of fact to be a cause which acts injuriously on health. Produced artificially by the accumulation of individuals in close tents, it may reasonably be supposed to produce its usual effects on armies. A cause of contagious influence, of fatal effect, is thus generated by accumulating soldiers in close and crowded tents, under the pretext of defending them from the inclemencies of the weather; and hence it is that the means which are provided for the preservation of health are actually the causes of destruction of life.

"There are two causes which more evidently act

upon the health of troops in the field than any other, namely, moisture exhaled direct from the surface of the earth in undue quantity, and emanations of a peculiar character arising from diseased action in the animal system in a mass of men crowded together. These are principal, and they are important. The noxious effects may be obviated, or rather the noxious cause will not be generated, under the following arrangement, namely, a carpet of painted canvas for the floor of the tent; a tent with a light roof, as defense against perpendicular rain or the rays of a vertical sun; and with side walls of moderate height, to be employed only against driving rains. To the first there can be no objection: it is useful, as preventing the exhalations of moisture from the surface of the earth; it is convenient, as always ready; and it is economical, as less expensive than straw. It requires to be fresh painted only once a year."

The effect of crowding men together in close quarters, illy ventilated, was shown in the prisons of Hindostan, where at one time, when the English held sway, they had, on an average, 40,000 natives in confinement; and this unfortunate population was every year liberated by death in proportions varying from 4000 to 10,000. The annual average mortality by crowded and unventilated barracks in the English army has sometimes been enormous, as at Barrackpore, where it seldom fell far short of one tenth; that is to say, its garrisons were every year decimated by fever or cholera, while the officers and other inhabitants, who lived in well-ventilated houses, did not find the place particularly unhealthy.

The same fact of general exemption among the officers, and complete exemption among their wives, was observed in the marching regiments, which lost by cholera from one tenth to one sixth of the enlisted men, who were packed together at night ten and twelve in a tent, with the thermometer at 96°. The dimensions of the celebrated Black Hole of Calcutta—where in 1756, 123 prisoners out of 140 died by carbonic acid in one night—was but eighteen feet square, and with but two small windows. Most of the twenty-three who survived until morning were seized with putrid fever and died very soon afterward.

On the 1st of December, 1848, 150 deck passengers of the steamer *Londonderry* were ordered below by the captain and the hatches closed upon them: seventy were found dead the next morning.

The streams which intersect our great prairies have but a very sparse growth of wood or vegetation upon their banks, so that one of the fundamental causes for the generation of noxious malaria does not, to any great extent, exist here, and I believe that persons may encamp with impunity directly upon their banks.

PICKET GUARDS.

When a party is sufficiently strong, a picket guard should be stationed during the night some two or three hundred yards in advance of the point which is most open to assault, and on low ground, so that an enemy approaching over the surrounding higher country can be seen against the sky, while the sentinel himself is screened from observation. These sentinels should not be allowed to keep fires, unless they are so placed that they cannot be seen from a distance.

During the day the pickets should be posted on the summits of the highest eminences in the vicinity of camp, with instructions to keep a vigilant lookout in all directions; and, if not within hailing distance, they should be instructed to give some well-understood telegraphic signals to inform those in camp when there is danger. For example, should Indians be discovered approaching at a great distance, they may raise their caps upon the muzzles of their pieces, and at the same time walk around in a circle; while, if the Indians are near and moving rapidly, the sentinel may swing his cap and run around rapidly in a circle. To indicate the direction from which the Indians are approaching, he may direct his piece toward them, and walk in the same line of direction.

Should the pickets suddenly discover a party of Indians very near, and with the apparent intention of making an attack, they should fire their pieces to give the alarm to the camp.

These telegraphic signals, when well understood and enforced, will tend greatly to facilitate the communication of intelligence throughout the camp, and conduce much to its security.

The picket guards should receive minute and strict orders regarding their duties under all circumstances, and these orders should be distinctly understood by everyone in the camp, so that no false alarms will be created. All persons, with the exception of the guards and herders, should after dark be confined to the limits of the chain of sentinels, so that, if anyone is seen approaching from without these limits, it will be known that they are strangers.

As there will not often be occasion for anyone to pass the chain of pickets during the night, it is a good rule (especially if the party is small), when a picket sentinel discovers anyone lurking about his post from without, if he has not himself been seen, to quietly withdraw and report the fact to the commander, who can wake his men and make his arrangements to repel an attack and protect his animals. If, however, the man upon the picket has been seen, he should distinctly challenge the approaching party, and if he receives no answer, fire, and retreat to camp to report the fact.

It is of the utmost importance that picket guards should be wide awake, and allow nothing to escape their observation, as the safety of the whole camp is involved. During a dark night a man can see better himself, and is less exposed to the view of others, when in a sitting posture than when standing up or moving about. I would therefore recommend this practice for night pickets.

Horses and mules (especially the latter), whose senses of hearing and smelling are probably more acute than those of almost any other animals, will discover anything strange or unusual about camp much sooner than a man. They indicate this by turning in the direction from whence the object is approaching, holding their heads erect, projecting their ears forward, and standing in a fixed and attentive attitude. They exhibit the same signs of alarm when a wolf or other wild animal approaches the camp; but it is always wise, when they show fear in this manner, to be on the alert till the cause is ascertained.

Mules are very keenly sensitive to danger, and, in passing along over the prairies, they will often detect the proximity of strangers long before they are discovered by their riders. Nothing seems to escape their observation; and I have heard of several instances where they have given timely notice of the approach of hostile Indians, and thus prevented stampedes.

Dogs are sometimes good sentinels, but they often sleep sound, and are not easily awakened on the approach of an enemy.

In marching with large force, unless there is a guide who knows the country, a small party should always be sent in advance to search for good camping places, and these parties should be dispatched early enough to return and meet the main command in the event of not finding a camping place within the limits of the day's march. A regiment should average upon the prairies, where the roads are good, about eighteen miles a day, but, if necessary, it can make 25 or even 30 miles. The advance party should therefore go as far as the command can march, provided the requisites for camping are not found within that distance. The article of first importance in campaigning is grass, the next water, and the last fuel.

It is the practice of most persons traveling with large ox trains to select their camps upon the summit of a hill, where the surrounding country in all directions can be seen. Their cattle are then continually within view from the camp, and can be guarded easily.

When a halt is made the wagons are "corraled," as it is called, by bringing the two front ones near and parallel to each other. The two next are then driven up on the outside of these, with the front wheels of the former touching the rear wheels of the latter, the rear of the wagons turned out upon the circumference of the circle that is being formed, and so on until one half the circle is made, when the rear of the wagons are turned in to complete the circle. An opening of about twenty yards should be left between the last two wagons for animals to pass in and out of the corral, and this may be closed with two ropes stretched between the wagons. Such a corral forms an excellent and secure barricade against Indian attacks, and a good enclosure for cattle while they are being yoked; indeed, it is indispensable.

STAMPEDES.

Enclosures are made in the same manner for horses and mules, and, in case of an attempt to stampede them, they should be driven with all possible dispatch into the corral, where they will be perfectly secure. A "stampede" is more to be dreaded upon the plains than almost any disaster that can happen. It not unfrequently occurs that very many animals are irretrievably lost in this way, and the objects of an expedition thus defeated.

The Indians are perfectly familiar with the habits and disposition of horses and mules, and with the most effectual methods of terrifying them. Previous to attempting a stampede, they provide themselves with rattles and other means for making frightful noises; thus prepared, they approach as near the herds as possible without being seen, and suddenly, with their horses at full speed, rush in among them, making the most hideous and unearthly screams and noises to terrify them, and drive them off before their astonished owners are able to rally and secure them.

As soon as the animals are started the Indians divide their party, leaving a portion to hurry them off rapidly, while the rest linger some distance in the rear, to resist those who may pursue them.

Horses and mules will sometimes, especially in the night, become frightened and stampeded from very slight causes. A wolf or a deer passing through a herd will often alarm them, and cause them to break away in the most frantic manner. Upon one occasion in the Choctaw country, my entire herd of about two hundred horses and mules all stampeded in the night, and scattered over the country for many miles, and it was several days before I succeeded in collecting them together. The alarm occurred while the herders were walking among the animals, and without any perceptible cause. The foregoing facts go to show how important it is at all times to keep a vigilant guard over animals. In the vicinity of hostile Indians, where an attack may be anticipated, several good horses should be secured in such positions that they will continually be in readiness for an emergency of this kind. The herdsmen should have their horses in hand, saddled and bridled, and ready at an instant's notice to spring upon their backs and drive the herds into camp. As soon as it is discovered that the animals have taken fright, the herdsmen should use their utmost endeavors to turn them in the direction of the camp, and this can generally be accomplished by riding the bell mare in front of the herd, and gradually turning her toward it, and slackening her speed as the familiar objects about the camp come in sight. This usually tends to quiet their alarm.

CHAPTER III.

Repairing broken Wagons.—Fording Rivers.—Quicksand.—Wagon Boats.—Bull Boats.—Crossing Packs.—Swimming Animals.—Marching with loose Horses.—Herding Mules.—Best Methods of Marching. —Herding and guarding Animals.—Descending Mountains.—Storms.—Northers.

REPAIRS OF ACCIDENTS.

THE ACCIDENTS most liable to happen to wagons on the plains arise from the great dryness of the atmosphere, and the consequent shrinkage and contraction of the woodwork in the wheels, the tires working loose, and the wheels, in passing over sidling ground, oftentimes falling down and breaking all the spokes where they enter the hub. It therefore becomes a matter of absolute necessity for the prairie traveler to devise some means of repairing such damages, or of guarding against them by the use of timely expedients.

The wheels should be frequently and closely examined, and whenever a tire becomes at all loose it should at once be tightened with pieces of hoop iron or wooden wedges driven by twos simultaneously from opposite sides. Another remedy for the same thing is to take off the wheels after encamping, sink them in water, and allow them to remain over night. This swells the wood, but is only temporary, requiring frequent repetition; and, after a time, if the wheels have not been made of thoroughly seasoned timber, it becomes necessary to reset the tires in order to guard against their destruction by falling to pieces and breaking the spokes.

If the tires run off near a blacksmith's shop, or if there be a traveling forge with the train, they may be tied on with raw hide or ropes, and thus driven to the shop or camp. When a rear wheel breaks down upon a march, the best method I know of for taking the vehicle to a place where it can be repaired is to take off the damaged wheel, and place a stout pole of three or four inches in diameter under the end of the axle, outside the wagon bed, and extending forward above the front wheel, where it is firmly lashed with ropes, while the other end of the pole runs six or eight feet to the rear, and drags upon the ground. The pole must be of such length and inclination that the axle shall be raised and retained in its proper horizontal position, when it can be driven to any distance that may be desired. The wagon should be relieved as much as practicable of its loading, as the pole dragging upon the ground will cause it to run heavily.

When a front wheel breaks down, the expedient just mentioned cannot be applied to the front axle, but the two rear wheels may be taken off and placed upon this axle (they will always fit), while the sound front wheel can be substituted upon one side of the rear axle, after which the pole may be applied as before described. This plan I have adopted upon several different occasions, and I can vouch for its efficacy.

The foregoing facts may appear very simple and unimportant in themselves, but blacksmiths and wheelwrights are not met with at every turn of the roads upon the prairies; and in the wilderness, where the traveler is dependent solely upon his own resources, this kind of information will be found highly useful.

When the spokes in a wheel shrink more than the felloes, they work loose in the hub, and cannot be tightened by wedging. The only remedy in such cases is to cut the felloe with a saw on opposite sides, taking out two pieces of such dimensions that the reduced circumference will draw back the spokes into their proper places and make them snug. A thin wagon-bow, or barrel hoops, may then be wrapped around the outside of the felloe, and secured with small nails or tacks. This increases the diameter of the wheel, so that when the tire has been heated, put on, and cooled, it forces back the spokes into their true places, and makes the wheel as sound and strong as it ever was. This simple process can be executed in about half an hour if there be fuel for heating, and obviates the necessity of cutting and welding the tire. I would recommend that the tires should be secured with bolts and nuts, which will prevent them from running off when they work loose, and, if they have been cut and re-set, they should be well tried with a hammer where they are welded to make sure that the junction is sound.

FORDING RIVERS.

Many streams that intersect the different routes across our continent are broad and shallow, and flow over beds of quicksand, which, in seasons of high water, become boggy and unstable, and are then exceedingly difficult of crossing. When these streams are on the rise, and, indeed, before any swelling is perceptible, their beds become surcharged with the sand loosened by the action of the undercurrent from the approaching flood, and from this time until the water subsides fording is difficult, requiring great precautions.

On arriving upon the bank of a river of this character which has not recently been crossed, the condition of the quicksand may be ascertained by sending an intelligent man over the fording place, and, should the sand not yield under his feet, it may be regarded as safe for animals or wagons. Should it, however, prove soft and yielding, it must be thoroughly examined, and the best track selected. This can be done by a man on foot, who will take a number of sharp sticks long enough, when driven into the bottom of the river, to stand above the surface of the water. He starts from the shore, and with one of the sticks and his feet tries the bottom in the direction of the opposite bank until he finds the firmest ground, where he plants one of the sticks to mark the track. A man incurs no danger in walking over quicksand provided he step rapidly, and he will soon detect the safest ground. He then proceeds, planting his sticks as often as may be necessary to mark the way, until he reaches the opposite bank. The ford is thus ascertained, and, if there are footmen in the party, they should cross before the animals and wagons, as they pack the sand, and make the track more firm and secure.

If the sand is soft, horses should be led across, and not allowed to stop in the stream; and the better to ensure this, they should be watered before entering upon the ford; otherwise, as soon as they stand still, their feet sink in the sand, and soon it becomes difficult to extricate them. The same rule holds in the passage of wagons: they must be driven steadily across, and the animals never allowed to stop while in the river, as the wheels sink rapidly in quicksand. Mules will often stop from fear, and, when once embarrassed in the sand, they lie down, and will not use the slightest exertion to regain their footing. The only alternative, then, is to drag them out with ropes. I have even known some mules refuse to put forth the least exertion to get up after being pulled out upon firm ground, and it was necessary to set them upon their feet before they were restored to a consciousness of their own powers.

In crossing rivers where the water is so high as to come into the wagon beds, but is not above a fording stage, the contents of the wagons may be kept dry by raising the beds between the uprights, and retaining them in that position with blocks of wood placed at each corner between the rockers and the bottom of the wagon beds. The blocks must be squared at each end, and their length, of course, should vary with the depth of water, which can be determined before cutting them. This is a very common and simple method of passing streams among emigrant travelers.

When streams are deep, with a very rapid current, it is difficult for the drivers to direct their teams to the proper coming-out places, as the current has a tendency to carry them too far down. This difficulty may be obviated by attaching a lariat rope to the leading animals, and having a mounted man ride in front with the rope in his hand, to assist the team in stemming the current, and direct it toward the point of egress. It is also a wise precaution, if the ford be at all hazardous, to place a mounted man on the lower side of the team with a whip, to urge forward any animal that may not work properly.

Where rivers are wide, with a swift current, they should always, if possible, be forded obliquely down stream, as the action of the water against the wagons assists very materially in carrying them across. In crossing the North Platte upon the Cherokee trail at a season when the water was high and very rapid, we were obliged to take the only practicable ford, which ran diagonally up the stream. The consequence was, that the heavy current, coming down with great force against the wagons, offered such powerful resistance to the efforts of the mules that it was with difficulty they could retain their footing, and several were drowned. Had the ford crossed obliquely down the river, there would have been no difficulty.

When it becomes necessary, with loaded wagons, to cross a stream of this character against the current, I would recommend that the teams be doubled, the leading animals led, a horseman placed on each side with whips to assist the driver, and that, before the first wagon enters the water, a man should be sent in advance to ascertain the best ford.

During seasons of high water, men, in traversing the plains, often encounter rivers which rise above a fording stage, and remain in that condition for many days, and to await the falling of the water might involve a great loss of time. If the traveler be alone, his only way is to swim his horse; but if he retains the seat on his saddle, his weight presses the animal down into the water, and cramps his movements very sensibly. It is a much better plan to attach a cord to the bridle bit, and drive him into the stream; then, seizing his tail, allow him to tow you across. If he turns out of the course, or attempts to turn back, he can be checked with the cord, or by

SWIMMING A HORSE

splashing water at his head. If the rider remains in the saddle, he should allow the horse to have a loose rein, and never pull upon it except when necessary to guide. If he wishes to steady himself, he can lay hold upon the mane.

In traveling with large parties, the following expedients for crossing rivers have been successfully resorted to within my own experience, and they are attended with no risk to life or property.

A rapid and deep stream, with high, abrupt, and soft banks, probably presents the most formidable array of unfavorable circumstances that can be found. Streams of this character are occasionally met with, and it is important to know how to cross them with the greatest promptitude and safety.

A train of wagons having arrived upon the bank of such a stream, first select the best point for the passage, where the banks upon both sides require the least excavation for a place of ingress and egress to and from the river. As I have before remarked, the place of entering the river should be above the coming-out place on the opposite bank, as the current will then assist in carrying wagons and animals across. A spot should be sought where the bed of the stream is firm at the place where the animals are to get out on the opposite bank. If, however, no such place can be found, brush and earth should be thrown in to make a foundation sufficient to support the animals, and to prevent them from bogging. After the place for crossing has been selected, it will be important to determine the breadth of the river between the points of ingress and egress, in order to show the length of rope necessary to reach across. A very simple practical method of doing this without instruments is found in the French "Manuel du Génie." It is as follows:

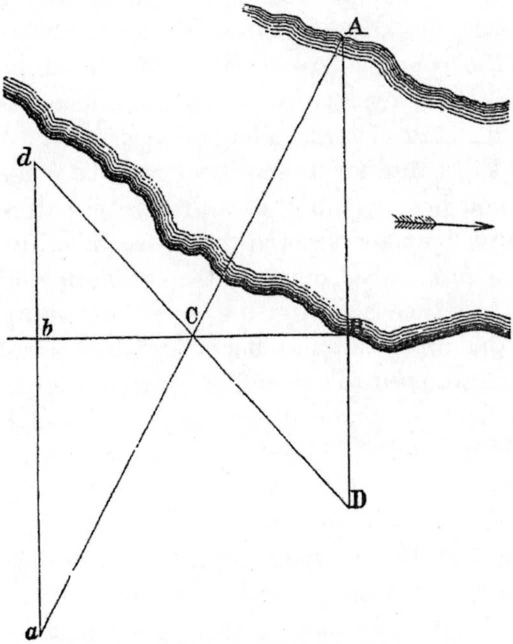

DIAGRAMS FOR MEASUREMENTS

The line AB (the distance to be measured) is extended upon the bank to D, from which point, after having marked it, lay off equal distances, DC and C*d*; produce BC to *b*, making CB=C*b*; then extend the line *db* until it intersects the prolongation of the line through CA at *a*. The distance between *ab* is equal to AB, or the width of the crossing.

A man who is an expert swimmer then takes the end of a fishing line or a small cord in his mouth, and carries it across, leaving the other end fixed upon the opposite bank, after which a lariat is attached to the cord, and one end of it pulled across and made fast to a tree; but if there is nothing convenient to which the lariat can be attached, an extra axle or coupling pole can be pulled over by the man who has crossed, firmly planted in the ground, and the rope tied to it. The rope must be long enough to extend twice across the stream, so that one end may always be left on each shore. A very good substitute for a ferry boat may be made with a wagon bed by filling it with empty water-casks, stopped tight and secured in the wagon with ropes, with a cask lashed opposite the center of each outside. It is then placed in the water bottom upward, and the rope that has been stretched across the stream attached to one end of it, while another rope is made fast to the other end, after which it is loaded, the shore end loosened, and the men on the opposite bank pull it across to the landing, where it is discharged and returned for another load, and so on until all the baggage and men are passed over.

The wagons can be taken across by fastening them down to the axles, attaching a rope to the end of the tongue, and another to the rear of each to steady it and hold it from drifting below the landing. It is then pushed into the stream, and the men on the opposite bank pull it over. I have passed a large train of wagons in this way across a rapid stream fifteen feet deep without any difficulty. I took, at the same time, a six-pounder cannon, which was separated from its carriage, and ferried over upon the wagon-boat; after which the carriage was pulled over in the same way as described for the wagons.

There are not always a sufficient number of air-tight water casks to fill a wagon bed, but a tent-fly, paulin, or wagon cover can generally be had. In this event, the wagon bed may be placed in the center of one of these, the cloth brought up around the ends and sides, and secured firmly with ropes tied around transversely, and another rope fastened lengthwise around under the rim. This holds the cloth in its place, and the wagon may then be placed in the water right side upward, and managed in the same manner as in the other case. If the cloth be made of cotton, it will soon swell so as to leak but very little, and answers a very good purpose.

Another method of ferrying streams is by means of what is called by the mountaineers a "bull-boat," the framework of which is made of willows bent into the shape of a short and wide skiff, with a flat bottom. Willows grow upon the banks of almost all the streams on the prairies, and can be bent into any shape desired. To make a boat with but one hide, a number of straight willows are cut about an inch in diameter, the ends sharpened and driven into the ground, forming a framework in the shape of a half eggshell cut through the longitudinal axis. Where these rods cross they are firmly secured with strings. A stout rod is then heated and bent around the frame in such a position that the edges of the hide, when laid over it and drawn tight, will just reach it. This rod forms the gunwale, which is secured by strings to the ribs. Small rods are then wattled in so as to make it symmetrical and strong. After which the green or soaked hide is thrown over the edges, sewed to the gunwales, and left to dry. The rods are then cut off even with the gunwale, and the boat is ready for use.

To build a boat with two or more hides: A stout pole of the desired length is placed upon the ground for a keel, the ends turned up and secured by a lariat; willow rods of the required dimensions are then cut, heated, and bent into the proper shape for knees, after which their centers are placed at equal distances upon the keel, and firmly tied with cords. The knees are retained in their proper curvature by cords around the ends. After a sufficient number of them have been placed upon the keel, two poles of suitable dimensions are heated, bent around the ends for a gunwale, and firmly lashed to each knee. Smaller willows are then interwoven, so as to model the frame.

Green or soaked hides are cut into the proper shape to fit the frame, and sewed together with buckskin strings; then the frame of the boat is placed in the middle, the hide drawn up snug around the sides, and secured with rawhide thongs to the gunwale. The boat is then turned bottom upward and left to dry, after which the seams where they have been sewed are covered with a mixture of melted tallow and pitch: the craft is now ready for launching.

A boat of this kind is very light and serviceable, but after a while becomes water-soaked, and should always be turned bottom upward to dry whenever it is not in the water. Two men can easily build a bull-boat of three hides in two days which will carry ten men with perfect safety.

A small party traveling with a pack train and arriving upon the banks of a deep stream will not always have the time to stop or the means to make any of the boats that have been described. Should their luggage be such as to become seriously injured by a wetting, and there be an India-rubber or gutta-percha cloth disposable, or if even a green beef or buffalo hide can be procured, it may be spread out upon the ground, and the articles of baggage placed in the center, in a square or rectangular form; the ends and sides are then brought up so as entirely to envelop the package, and the whole secured with ropes or raw hide. It is then placed in the water with a rope attached to one end, and towed across by men in the same manner as the boats before described. If hides be used they will require greasing occasionally, to prevent their becoming water-soaked.

When a mounted party with pack animals arrive upon the borders of a rapid stream, too deep to ford, and where the banks are high and abrupt, with perhaps but one place where the beasts can get out upon the opposite shore, it would not be safe to drive or ride them in, calculating that all will make the desired landing. Some of them will probably be carried by the swift current too far down the stream, and thereby endanger not only their own lives, but the lives of their riders. I have seen the experiment tried repeatedly, and have known several animals to be carried by the current below the point of egress, and thus drowned. Here is a simple, safe, and expeditious method of taking animals over such a stream. Suppose, for example, a party of mounted men arrive upon the bank of the stream. There will always be some good swimmers in the party, and probably others who cannot swim at all. Three or four of the most expert of these are selected, and sent across with one end of a rope made of lariats tied together, while the other end is retained upon the first bank, and made fast to the neck of a gentle and good swimming horse; after which another gentle horse is brought up and made fast by a lariat around his neck to the tail of the first, and so on until all the horses are thus tied together. The men who cannot swim are then mounted upon the best swimming horses and tied on, otherwise they are liable to become frightened, lose their balance, and be carried away in a rapid

CROSSING A STREAM

current; or a horse may stumble and throw his rider. After the horses have been strung out in a single line by their riders, and everything is in readiness, the first horse is lead carefully into the water, while the men on the opposite bank, pulling upon the rope, thus direct him across, and, if necessary, aid him in stemming the current. As soon as this horse strikes bottom he pulls upon those behind him, and thereby assists them in making the landing, and in this manner all are passed over in perfect safety.

DRIVING LOOSE HORSES.

In traveling with loose horses across the plains, some persons are in the habit of attaching them in pairs by their halters to a long, stout rope stretched between two wagons drawn by mules, each wagon being about half loaded. The principal object of the rear wagon being to hold back and keep the rope stretched, not more than two stout mules are required, as the horses aid a good deal with their heads in pulling this wagon. From thirty to forty horses may be driven very well in this manner, and, if they are wild, it is perhaps the safest method, except that of leading them with halters held by men riding beside them. The rope to which the horses are attached should be about an inch and a quarter in diameter, with loops or rings inserted at intervals sufficient to admit the horses without allowing them to kick each other, and the halter straps tied to these loops. The horses, on first starting, should have men by their sides, to accustom them to this manner of being led. The wagons should be so driven as to keep the rope continually stretched. Good drivers must be assigned to these wagons, who will constantly watch the movements of the horses attached, as well as their own teams.

I have had 150 loose horses driven by ten mounted herdsmen. This requires great care for some considerable time, until the horses become gentle and accustomed to their herders. It is important to ascertain, as soon as possible after starting, which horses are wild, and may be likely to stampede and lead off the herd; such should be led, and never suffered to run loose, either on the march or in camp. Animals of this character will soon indicate their propensities, and can be secured during the first days of the march. It is desirable that all animals that will not stampede when not working should run loose on a march, as they pick up a good deal of grass along the road when traveling, and the success of an expedition, when animals get no other forage but grass, depends in a great degree upon the time given them for grazing. They will thrive much better when allowed a free range than when picketed, as they then are at liberty to select such grass as suits them. It may therefore be set down as an infallible rule never to be departed from, that all animals, excepting such as will be likely to stampede, should be turned loose for grazing immediately after arriving at the camping place; but it is equally important that they should be carefully herded as near the camp as good grass will admit; and those that it is necessary to picket should be placed upon the best grass, and their places changed often. The ropes to which they are attached should be about forty feet long; the picket pins, of iron, fifteen inches long, with ring and swivel at top, so that the rope shall not twist as the animal feeds around it; and the pins must be firmly driven into tenacious earth.

Animals should be herded during the day at such distances as to leave sufficient grass undisturbed around and near the camp for grazing through the night.

METHOD OF MARCHING.

Among men of limited experience in frontier life will be found a great diversity of opinion regarding the best methods of marching, and of treating animals in expeditions upon the prairies. Some will make late starts and travel during the heat of the day without nooning, while others will start early and make two marches, laying by during the middle of the day; some will picket their animals continually in camp, while others will herd them day and night, etc., etc. For mounted troops, or, indeed, for any body of men traveling with horses and mules, a few general rules may be specified which have the sanction of mature experience, and a deviation from them will inevitably result in consequences highly detrimental to the best interests of an expedition.

In ordinary marches through a country where grass and water are abundant and good, animals receiving proper attention should not fall away, even if they receive no grain; and, as I said before, they should not be made to travel faster than a walk unless absolutely necessary; neither should they be taken off the road for the purpose of hunting or chasing buffalo, as one buffalo-chase injures them more than a week of moderate riding. In the vicinity of hostile Indians, the animals must be carefully herded and guarded within protection of the camp, while those picketed should be changed as often as the grass is eaten off within the circle described by the tether rope. At night they should be brought within the chain of sentinels and picketed as compactly as is consistent with the space needed for grazing, and under no circumstances, unless the Indians are known to be near and an attack is to be expected, should they be tied up to a picket line where they can get no grass. Unless allowed to graze at night they will fall away rapidly, and soon become unserviceable. It is much better to march after nightfall, turn some distance off the road, and to encamp without fires in a depressed locality where the Indians cannot track the party, and the animals may be picketed without danger.

In descending abrupt hills and mountains one wheel of a loaded wagon should always be locked, as this relieves the wheel animals and makes everything more secure. When the declivity is great both rear wheels should be locked, and if very abrupt, requiring great effort on the wheel animals to hold the wagon, the wheels should be rough-locked by lengthening the lock chains so that the part which goes around the wheels will come directly upon the ground, and thus create more friction. Occasionally, however, hills are met with so nearly perpendicular that it becomes necessary to attach ropes to the rear axle, and to station men to hold back upon them and steady the vehicle down the descent. Rough-locking is a very safe method of passing heavy artillery down abrupt declivities. There are several mountains between the Missouri River and California where it is necessary to resort to one of the two last-mentioned methods in order to descend with security. If there are no lock chains upon wagons, the front and rear wheels on the same side may be tied together with ropes so as to lock them very firmly.

It is an old and well-established custom among men experienced in frontier life always to cross a stream upon which it is intended to encamp for the night, and this rule should never be departed from where a stream is to be forded, as a rise during the night might detain the traveler for several days in awaiting the fall of the waters.

STORMS.

In Western Texas, during the autumn and winter months, storms arise very suddenly, and, when accompanied by a north wind, are very severe upon men and animals; indeed, they are sometimes so terrific as to make it necessary for travelers to hasten to the nearest sheltered place to save the lives of their animals. When these storms come from the north, they are called "northers"; and as, during the winter season, the temperature often undergoes a sudden change of many degrees at the time the storm sets in, the perspiration is checked, and the system receives an instantaneous shock, against which it requires great vital energy to bear up. Men and animals are not, in this mild climate, prepared for these capricious meteoric revolutions, and they not unfrequently perish under their effects.

While passing near the headwaters of the Colorado in October 1849, I left one of my camps at an early hour in the morning under a mild and soft atmosphere, with a gentle breeze from the south, but had marched only a short distance when the wind suddenly whipped around into the north, bringing with it a furious chilling rain, and in a short time the road became so soft and heavy as to make the labor of pulling the wagons over it very exhausting upon the mules, and they came into camp in a profuse sweat, with the rain pouring down in torrents upon them.

They were turned out of harness into the most sheltered place that could be found; but, instead of eating, as was their custom, they turned their heads from the wind, and remained in that position, chilled and trembling, without making the least effort to move. The rain continued with unabated fury during the entire day and night, and on the following morning thirty-five out of one hundred and ten mules had perished, while those remaining could hardly be said to have had a spark of vitality left. They were drawn up with the cold, and could with difficulty walk. Tents and wagon covers were cut up to protect them, and they were then driven about for some time, until a little vital energy was restored, after which they commenced eating grass, but it was three or four days before they recovered sufficiently to resume the march.

The mistake I made was in driving the mules after the "norther" commenced. Had I gone immediately into camp, before they became heated and wearied, they would probably have eaten the grass, and this, I have no doubt, would have saved them; but as it was, their blood became heated from overwork, and the sudden chill brought on a reaction which proved fatal. If an animal will eat his forage plentifully, there is but little danger of his perishing with cold. This I assert with much confidence, as I once, when traveling with about 1500 horses and mules, encountered the most terrific snowstorm that has been known within the memory of the oldest mountaineers. It commenced on the last day of April, and continued without cessation for sixty consecutive hours. The day had been mild and pleasant; the green grass was about six inches high; the trees had put out their new leaves, and all nature conspired to show that the somber garb of winter had been permanently superseded by the smiling attire of spring. About dark, however, the wind turned into the north; it commenced to snow violently, and increased until it became a frightful tempest, filling the atmosphere with a dense cloud of driving snow, against which it was impossible to ride or walk. Soon after the storm set in, one herd of three hundred horses and mules broke away from the herdsmen who were around them, and, in spite of all their efforts, ran at full speed, directly with the wind and snow, for fifty miles before they stopped.

Three of the herdsmen followed them as far as they were able, but soon became exhausted and lost on the prairie. One of them found his way back to camp in a state of great prostration and suffering. One of the others was found dead, and the third crawling about upon his hands and knees, after the storm ceased.

It happened, fortunately, that I had reserved a quantity of corn to be used in the event of finding a scarcity of grass, and as soon as the ground became covered with snow, so that the animals could not get at the grass, I fed out the corn, which I am induced to believe saved their lives. Indeed, they did not seem to be at all affected by this prolonged and unseasonable tempest. This occurred upon the summit of the elevated ridge dividing the waters of the Arkansas and South Platte rivers, where storms are said to be of frequent occurrence.

The greater part of the animals that stampeded were recovered after the storm, and, although they had traveled a hundred miles at a very rapid pace, they did not seem to be much affected by it.

CHAPTER IV.

Packing. —Saddles. —Mexican Method. —Madrina, or Bellmare. —Attachment of the Mule illustrated. —Best Method of Packing. —Hoppling Animals. —Selecting Horses and Mules. —Grama and bunch Grass. —European Saddles. —California Saddle. —Saddle Wounds. —Alkali. —Flies. —Colic. —Rattlesnake Bites. —Cures for the Bite.

PACKING AND DRIVING

With a train of pack animals properly organized and equipped, a party may travel with much comfort and celerity. It is enabled to take shortcuts, and move over the country in almost any direction without regard to roads. Mountains and broken ground may easily be traversed, and exemption is gained from many of the troubles and detentions attendant upon the transit of cumbersome wagon trains.

One of the most essential requisites to the outfit of a pack train is a good packsaddle. Various patterns are in use, many of which are mere instruments of torture upon the backs of the poor brutes, lacerating them cruelly, and causing continued pain.

The Mexicans use a leathern packsaddle without a tree. It is stuffed with hay, and is very large, covering almost the entire back, and extending far down the sides. It is secured with a broad hair girth, and the load is kept in position by a lash rope drawn by two men so tight as to give the unfortunate beast intense suffering.

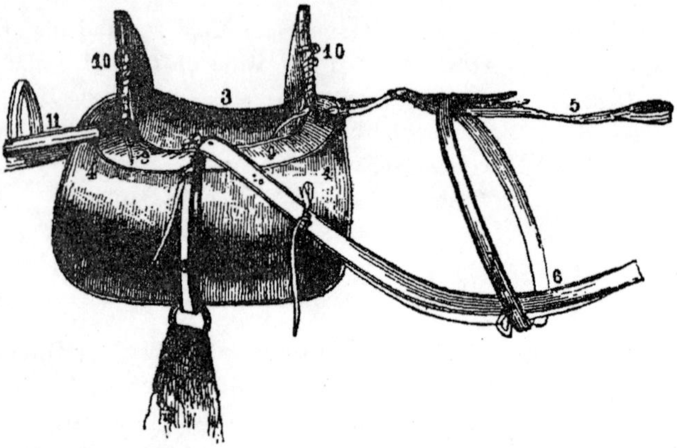

GRIMSLEY'S PACK-SADDLE.

A packsaddle is made by T. Grimsley, No. 41 Main Street, St. Louis, Mo. It is open at the top, with a light, compact, and strong tree, which fits the animal's back well, and is covered with rawhide, put on green, and drawn tight by the contraction in drying. It has a leathern breast-strap, breeching, and lash strap, with a broad hair girth fastened in the Mexican fashion. Of sixty-five of these saddles that I used in crossing the Rocky Mountains, over an exceedingly rough and broken section, not one of them wounded a mule's back, and I regard them as the best saddles I have ever seen.

No people, probably, are more familiar with the art of packing than the Mexicans. They understand the habits, disposition, and powers of the mule perfectly, and will get more work out of him than any other men I have ever seen. The mule and the donkey are to them as the camel to the Arab—their porters over deserts and mountains where no other means of transportation can be used to advantage. The Spanish Mexicans are, however, cruel masters, having no mercy upon their beasts, and it is no uncommon thing for them to load their mules with the enormous burden of three or four hundred pounds.

These muleteers believe that, when the pack is firmly lashed, the animal supports his burden better and travels with greater ease, which seems quite probable, as the tension forms, as it were, an external sheath supporting and bracing the muscles. It also has a tendency to prevent the saddle from slipping and chafing the mule's back. With such huge *cargas* as the Mexicans load upon their mules, it is impossible, by any precautions, to prevent their back and withers from becoming horribly mangled, and it is common to see them working their animals day after day in this miserable plight. This heavy packing causes the scars that so often mark Mexican mules.

The animal, in starting out from camp in the morning, groaning under the weight of his heavy burden, seems hardly able to move; but the pack soon settles, and so loosens the lashing that after a short time he moves along with more ease. Constant care and vigilance on the part of the muleteers are necessary to prevent the packs from working loose and falling off. The adjustment of a *carga* upon a mule does not, however, detain the caravan, as the others move on while it is being righted. If the mules are suffered to halt, they are apt to lie down, and it is very difficult for them, with their loads, to rise; besides, they are likely to strain themselves in their efforts to do so. The Mexicans, in traveling with large caravans, usually make the day's march without nooning, as too much time would be consumed in unloading and packing up again.

Packs, when taken off in camp, should be piled in a row upon the ground, and, if there be a prospect of rain, the saddles should be placed over them, and the whole covered with the saddle blankets or canvas.

The muleteers and herders should be mounted upon well-trained horses, and be careful to keep the animals of the caravan from wandering or scattering along the road. This can easily be done by having some of the men riding upon each side, and others in rear of the caravan.

In herding mules it is customary among prairie travelers to have a bell-mare, to which the mules soon become so attached that they will follow her wherever she goes. By keeping her in charge of one of the herdsmen, the herds are easily controlled; and during a stampede, if the herdsman mounts her, and rushes ahead toward camp, they will generally follow.

In crossing rivers the bell-mare should pass first, after which the mules are easily induced to take to the water and pass over, even if they have to swim. Mules are good swimmers unless they happen, by plunging off a high bank, to get water in their ears, when they are often drowned. Whenever a mule in the water drops his ears, it is a sure indication that he has water in them, and he should be taken out as soon as possible. To prevent accidents of this nature, where the water is deep and the banks abrupt, the mule herds should be allowed to enter slowly, and without crowding, as otherwise they are not only likely to get their heads under water, but to throw each other over and get injured.

The *madrina,* or bell-mare, acts a most important part in a herd of mules, and is regarded by experienced campaigners as indispensable to their security. She is selected for her quiet and regular habits. She will not wander far from the camp. If she happen to have a colt by her side, this is no objection, as the mules soon form the most devoted attachment to it. I have often seen them leave their grazing when very hungry, and flock around a small colt, manifesting their delight by rubbing it with their noses, licking it with their tongues, kicking up their heels, and making a variety of other grotesque demonstrations of affection, while the poor little colt, perfectly unconscious of the cause of these ungainly caresses, stood trembling with fear, but unable to make his escape from the compact circle of his mulish admirers. Horses and asses are also used as bell animals, and the mules soon become accustomed to following them. If a man leads or rides a bell animal in advance, the mules follow, like so many dogs, in the most orderly procession.

"After traveling about fourteen miles," says Bayard Taylor, "we were joined by three miners, and our mules, taking a sudden liking for their horses, jogged on at a more brisk pace. The instincts of the mulish heart form an interesting study to the traveler in the mountains. I would (were the comparison not too ungallant) liken it to a woman's, for it is quite as uncertain in its sympathies, bestowing its affections when least expected, and, when bestowed, quite as constant, so long as the object is not taken away. Sometimes a horse, sometimes an ass, captivates the fancy of a whole drove of mules, but often an animal nowise akin. Lieutenant Beale told me that his whole train of mules once galloped off suddenly, on the plains of the Cimarone, and ran half a mile, when they halted in apparent satisfaction. The cause of their freak was found to be a buffalo calf which had strayed from the herd. They were frisking around it in the greatest delight, rubbing their noses against it, throwing up their heels, and making themselves ridiculous by abortive attempts to neigh and bray, while the calf, unconscious of its attractive qualities, stood trembling in their midst."

"If several large troops," says Charles Darwin, "are turned into one field to graze in the morning, the muleteer has only to lead the *madrinas* a little apart and tinkle their bells, and, although there may be 200 or 300 mules together, each immediately knows its own bell, and separates itself from the rest. The affection of these animals for their madrina saves infinite trouble. It is nearly impossible to lose an old mule, for, if detained several hours by force, she will, by the power of smell, like a dog, track out her companions, or rather the madrina; for, according to the muleteer, she is the chief object of affection. The feeling, however, is not of an individual nature, for I believe I am right in saying that any animal with a bell will serve as a madrina."

Of the attachment that a mule will form for a horse, I will cite an instance from my own observation, which struck me at the time as being one of the most remarkable and touching evidences of devotion that I have ever known among the brute creation.

On leaving Fort Leavenworth with the army for Utah in 1857, one of the officers rode a small mule, whose kind and gentle disposition soon caused him to become a favorite among the soldiers, and they named him "Billy." As this officer and myself were often thrown together upon the march, the mule, in the course of a few days, evinced a growing attachment for a mare that I rode. The sentiment was not, however, reciprocated on her part, and she intimated as much by the reversed position of her ears, and the free exercise of her feet and teeth whenever Billy came within her reach; but these signal marks of displeasure, instead of discouraging, rather seemed to increase his devotion, and whenever at liberty he invariably sought to get near her, and appeared much distressed when not permitted to follow her.

On leaving Camp Scott for New Mexico Billy was among the number of mules selected for the expedition. During the march I was in the habit, when starting out from camp in the morning, of leading off the party, and directing the packmen to hold the mule until I should get so far in advance with the mare that he could not see us; but the moment he was released he would, in spite of all the efforts of the packers, start off at a most furious pace, and never stop or cease braying until he reached the mare's side. We soon found it impossible to keep him with the other mules, and he was finally permitted to have his own way.

In the course of time we encountered the deep snows in the Rocky Mountains, where the animals could get no forage, and Billy, in common with the others, at length became so weak and jaded that he was unable any longer to leave his place in the caravan and break a track through the snow around to the front. He made frequent attempts to turn out and force his way ahead, but after numerous unsuccessful efforts he would fall down exhausted, and set up a most mournful braying.

The other mules soon began to fail, and to be left, worn out and famished, to die by the wayside; it was not, however, for some time that Billy showed symptoms of becoming one of the victims, until one evening after our arrival at camp I was informed that he had dropped down and been left upon the road during the day. The men all deplored his loss exceedingly, as his devotion to the mare had touched their kind hearts, and many expressions of sympathy were uttered around their bivouac fires on that evening.

Much to our surprise, however, about ten o'clock, just as we were about going to sleep, we heard a mule braying about half a mile to the rear upon our trail. Sure enough, it proved to be Billy, who, after having rested, had followed upon our track and overtaken us. As soon as he reached the side of the mare he lay down and seemed perfectly contented.

The next day I relieved him from his pack, and allowed him to run loose; but during the march he gave out, and was again abandoned to his fate, and this time we certainly never expected to see him more. To our great astonishment, however, about twelve o'clock that night the sonorous but not very musical notes of Billy in the distance aroused us from our slumbers, and again announced his approach. In an instant the men were upon their feet, gave three hearty cheers, and rushed out in a body to meet and escort him into camp.

But this well-meant ovation elicited no response from him. He came reeling and floundering along through the deep snow, perfectly regardless of these honors, pushing aside all those who occupied the trail or interrupted his progress in the least, wandered about until he found the mare, dropped down by her side, and remained until morning.

When we resumed our march on the following day he made another desperate effort to proceed, but soon fell down exhausted, when we reluctantly abandoned him, and saw him no more.

Alas! poor Billy! your constancy deserved a better fate; you may, indeed, be said to have been a victim to unrequited affection.

The articles to be transported should be made up into two packages of precisely equal weight, and as nearly equal in bulk as practicable, otherwise they will sway the saddle over to one side, and cause it to chafe the animal's back.

The packages made, two ropes about six feet long are fastened around the ends by a slipknot, and if the packages contain corn or other articles that will shift about, small sticks should be placed between the sacks and the ropes, which equalizes the pressure and keeps the packages snug. The ropes are then looped at the ends, and made precisely of the same length, so that the packs will balance and come up well toward the top of the saddle. Two men then, each taking a pack, go upon opposite sides of the mule, that has been previously saddled, and, raising the packs simultaneously, place the loops over the pommel and cantel, settling them well down into their places. The lashing strap is then thrown over the top, brought through the rings upon each side, and drawn as tight at every turn as the two men on the sides can pull it, and, after having been carried back and forth diagonally across the packs as often as its length admits (generally three or four times), it is made fast to one of the rings, and securely tied in a slipknot.

The breast strap and breeching must not be buckled so close as to chafe the skin; the girth should be broad and soft where it comes opposite the forelegs, to prevent cutting them. Leather girths should be wrapped with cloth or bound with soft material. The hair girth, being soft and elastic, is much better than leather.

The crupper should never be dispensed with in a mountainous country, but it must be soft, round, and about an inch in diameter where it comes in contact with the tail, otherwise it will wound the animal in making long and abrupt descents.

In Norway they use a short round stick, about ten inches long, which passes under the tail, and from each end of this a cord connects with the saddle.

Camp kettles, tin vessels, and other articles that will rattle and be likely to frighten animals, should be firmly lashed to the packs. When the packs work loose, the lash strap should be untied, and a man upon each side draw it up again and make it fast. When ropes are used for lashing, they may be tightened by twisting them with a short stick and making the stick fast.

One hundred and twenty-five pounds is a sufficient load for a mule upon a long journey.

In traveling over a rocky country, and upon all long journeys, horses and mules should be shod, to prevent their hoofs wearing out or breaking. The mountaineers contend that beasts travel better without shoeing, but I have several times had occasion to regret the omission of this very necessary precaution. A few extra shoes and nails, with a small hammer, will enable travelers to keep their animals shod.

In turning out pack animals to graze, it is well either to keep the lariat ropes upon them with the ends trailing upon the ground, or to hopple them, as no corral can be made into which they may be driven in order to catch them. A very good way to catch an animal without driving him into an enclosure is for two men to take a long rope and stretch it out at the height of the animal's neck; some men then drive him slowly up against it, when one of the men with the rope runs around behind the animal and back to the front again, thus taking a turn with the rope around his neck and holding him secure.

To prevent an animal from kicking, take a forked stick and make the forked part fast to the bridle bit, bringing the two ends above the head and securing them there, leaving the part of the stick below the fork of sufficient length to reach near the ground when the animal's head is in its natural position. He cannot kick up unless he lowers his head, and the stick effectually prevents that.

Tether ropes should be so attached to the neck of the animal as not to slip and choke him, and the picket pins never be left on the ropes except when in the ground, as, in the event of a stampede, they are very likely to swing around and injure the animals.

Many experienced travelers were formerly in the habit of securing their animals with a strap or iron ring fastened around the fetlock of one forefoot, and this attached to the tether rope. This method holds the animal very securely to the picket pin, but when the rope is first put on, and before he becomes accustomed to it, he is liable to throw himself down and get hurt; so that I think the plan of tethering by the neck or halter is the safest, and, so far as I have observed, is now universally practiced.

The mountaineers and Indians seldom tether their animals, but prefer the plan of hoppling, as this gives them more latitude for ranging and selecting the choicest grass.

Two methods of hoppling are practiced among the Indians and hunters of the West: one with a strap about two feet long buckling around the fore-legs above the fetlock joints; the other is what they term the "side hopple," which is made by buckling a strap around a front and rear leg upon the same side. In both cases care should be taken not to buckle the strap so tight as to chafe the legs. The latter plan is the best, because the animal, side-hoppled, is able to go but little faster than a walk, while the front hopple permits him, after a little practice, to gallop off at considerable speed. If the hopples are made of iron connected with chains, like handcuffs, with locks and keys, it will be impossible for the Indians, without files, to cut them; but the parts that come in contact with the legs should be covered with soft leather.

"A horse," says Mr. Galton, "may be hoppled with a stirrup-leather by placing the middle around one leg, then twisting it several times and buckling it round the other leg. When you wish to picket horses in the middle of a sandy plain, dig a hole two or three feet deep, and, tying your rope to a fagot of sticks or brushwood, or even to a bag filled with sand, bury this in it."

For prairie service, horses which have been raised exclusively upon grass, and never been fed on grain, or "range horses," as they are called in the West, are decidedly the best, and will perform more hard labor than those that have been stabled and groomed. The large, stout ponies found among some of our frontier settlements are well adapted to this service, and endure admirably. The same remarks hold good in the choice of mules; and it will be found that the square-built, big-bellied, and short legged Mexican mule will endure far more hard service, on short allowance of forage, than the larger American mule which has been accustomed to grain.

In our trip across the Rocky Mountains we had both the American and Mexican mules, and improved a good opportunity of giving their relative powers of endurance a thorough service-trial. For many days they were reduced to a meager allowance of dry grass, and at length got nothing but pine leaves, while their work in the deep snow was exceedingly severe. This soon told upon the American mules, and all of them, with the exception of two, died, while most of the Mexican mules went through. The result was perfectly conclusive.

We found that, where the snow was not more than two feet deep, the animals soon learned to paw it away and get at the grass. Of course they do not get sufficient in this way, but they do much better than one would suppose.

In Utah and New Mexico the autumn is so dry that the grass does not lose its nutritious properties by being washed with rains. It gradually dries and cures like hay, so that animals eat it freely, and will fatten upon it even in midwinter. It is seldom that any grain is fed to stock in either of these territories.

Several of the varieties of grass growing upon the slopes of the Rocky Mountains are of excellent quality; among these may be mentioned the Gramma and bunch grasses. Horses and mules turned out to graze always prefer the grass upon the mountain sides to grass of the valleys.

We left New Mexico about the first of March, six weeks before the new grass appeared, with 1500 animals, many of them low in flesh, yet they improved upon the journey, and on their arrival in Utah were all, with very few exceptions, in fine working condition. Had this march been made at the same season in the country bordering upon the Missouri River, where there are heavy autumnal rains, the animals would probably have become very poor.

In this journey the herds were allowed to range over the best grass that could be found, but were guarded both night and day with great care, whereas, if they had been corraled or picketed at night, I daresay they would have lost flesh.*

SADDLES.

Great diversity of opinion exists regarding the best equipment for horses, and the long-mooted question is as yet very far from being definitely settled.

I do not regard the opinions of Europeans as having a more direct bearing upon this question, or as

* Some curious and interesting experiments are said to have been recently made at the veterinary school at Alfort, near Paris, by order of the minister of war, to ascertain the powers of endurance of horses. It appears that a horse will live on water alone five-and-twenty days; seventeen days without eating or drinking; only five days if fed and unwatered; ten days if fed and insufficiently watered. A horse kept without water for three days drank one hundred and four pounds of water in three minutes. It was found that a horse taken immediately after "feed," and kept in the active exercise of the "squadron school," completely digested its "feed" in three hours; in the same time in the "conscript's school" its food was two thirds digested; and if kept perfectly quiet in the stable, its digestion was scarcely commenced in three hours.

tending to establish any more definite and positive conclusions regarding it than have been developed by the experience of our own border citizens, the major part of whose lives has been spent in the saddle; yet I am confident that the following brief description of the horse equipments used in different parts of Europe, the substance of which I have extracted from Captain M'Clellan's interesting report, will be read with interest and instruction.

The saddle used by the African chasseurs consists of a plain wooden tree, with a pad upon the top, but without skirts, and is somewhat similar to our own military saddle, but lower in the pommel and cantle. The girth and surcingle are of leather, with an ordinary woolen saddle blanket. Their bridle has a single headstall, with the Spanish bit buckled to it.

A new saddle has recently been introduced into the French service by Captain Cogent, the tree of which is cut out of a single piece of wood, the cantle only being glued on, and a piece of walnut let into the pommel, with a thin strip veneered upon the front ends of the bars. The pommel and cantle are lower than in the old model; the whole is covered with wet rawhide, glued on and sewed at the edges. The great advantage this saddle possesses is in being so arranged that it may be used for horses of all sizes and conditions. The saddle blanket is made of thick felt cloth, and is attached to the pommel by a small strap passing through holes in the blanket, which is thus prevented from slipping, and at the same time it raises the saddle so as to admit a free circulation of air over the horse's spine.

The Hungarian saddle is made of hard wood entirely uncovered, with a raised pommel and cantle. The seat is formed with a leather strap four inches wide nailed to the forks on the front and rear, and secured to the side boards by leather thongs, thus giving an elastic and easy saddle seat. This is also the form of the saddletree used by the Russian and Austrian cavalry. The Russians have a leather girth fastened by three small buckles: it passes over the tree, and is tied to the side boards. The saddle blanket is of stout felt cloth in four thicknesses, and a layer of black leather over it, and the whole held together by leather thongs passing through and through. When the horse falls off in flesh, more thicknesses are added, and vice versa. This saddle blanket is regarded by the Russian officers as the best possible arrangement. The Russians use the curb and snaffle bits made of steel.

The Cossack saddle has a thick padding under the side boards and on the seat, which raises the rider very high on his horse, so that his feet are above the bottom of the belly. Their bridle has but a simple snaffle bit, and no martingale.

The Prussian cuirassiers have a heavy saddle with a low pommel and cantle, covered with leather, but it is not thought by Captain M'Clellan to present anything worthy of imitation.

The other Prussian cavalry ride the Hungarian

saddle, of a heavier model than the one in the Austrian service. The surcingle is of leather, and fastens in the Mexican style; the girth is also of leather, three and a half inches wide, with a large buckle. It is in two parts, attached to the bars by rawhide thongs. The curb and snaffle steel bits are used, and attached to a single headstall.

The English cavalry use a saddle which has a lower cantle and pommel than our *Grimsley saddle*, covered with leather. The snaffle bit is attached to the halter headstall by a chain and T; the curb has a separate headstall, which on a march is occasionally taken off and hung on the carbine stock.

The Sardinian saddle has a bare wooden tree very similar to the Hungarian. A common blanket, folded in twelve thicknesses, is placed under it. The girth and surcingle are of leather.

Without expressing any opinion as to the comparative merits of these different saddles, I may be permitted to give a few general principles, which I regard as infallible in the choice of a saddle.

The side boards should be large, and made to conform to the shape of the horse's back, thereby distributing the burden over a large surface. It should stand up well above the spine, so as to admit a free circulation of air under it.

For long journeys, the crupper, where it comes in contact with the tail, should be made of soft leather. It should be drawn back only far enough to hold the saddle from the withers. Some horses require much more tension upon the crupper than others. The girth should be made broad, of a soft and elastic material. Those made of hair, in use among the Mexicans, fulfill the precited conditions.

A light and easy bit, which will not fret or chafe the horse, is recommended.

The saddle blanket must be folded even and smooth, and placed on so as to cover every part of the back that comes in contact with the saddle, and in warm weather it is well to place a gunny bag under the blanket, as it is cooler than the wool.

It will have been observed that, in the French service, the folded saddle blanket is tied to the pommel to prevent it slipping back. This is well if the blanket be taken off and thoroughly dried whenever the horse is unsaddled.

A saddle blanket made of moss is used in some of the Southwestern States, which is regarded by many as the perfection of this article of horse equipment. It is a mat woven into the proper shape and size from the beaten fibers of moss that hangs from the trees in our Southern States. It is cheap, durable, is not in any way affected by sweat, and does not chafe or heat the horse's spine like the woolen blanket. Its open texture allows a rapid evaporation, which tends to keep the back cool, and obviates the danger of stripping and sudden exposure of the heated parts to the sun and air.

The experience of some of our officers who have used this mat for years in Mexico and Texas corroborates all I have said in its favor; and they are unanimous in the opinion that a horse will never get a sore back when it is placed under a good saddle.

A saddle made by the Mexicans in California is called the *California saddle.* This is extensively used upon the Pacific slope of the mountains, and is believed to possess, at least, as many advantages for rough frontier service as any other pattern that has been invented. Those hardy and experienced veterans, the mountaineers, could not be persuaded to ride any other saddle, and their ripened knowledge of such matters certainly gives weight to their conclusions.

CALIFORNIA SADDLE.

The merits of the California saddle consist in its being light, strong, and compact, and conforming well to the shape of the horse. When strapped on, it rests so firmly in position that the strongest pull of a horse upon a lariat attached to the pommel cannot displace it. Its shape is such that the rider is compelled to sit nearly erect, with his legs on the continuation of the line of the body, which makes his seat more secure, and, at the same time, gives him a better control over his arms and horse. This position is attained by setting the stirrup leathers farther back than on the old-fashioned saddle. The pommel is high, like the Mexican saddle, and prevents the rider from being thrown forward. The tree is covered with rawhide, put on green, and sewed; when this dries and contracts it gives it great strength. It has no iron in its composition, but is kept together by buckskin strings, and can easily be taken to pieces for mending or cleaning. It has a hair girth about five inches wide.

The whole saddle is covered with a large and thick sheet of sole leather, having a hole to lay over the pommel; it extends back over the horse's hips, and protects them from rain, and when taken off in camp it furnishes a good security against dampness when placed under the traveler's bed.

The California saddletree is regarded by many as the best of all others for the horse's back, and as having an easier seat than the Mexican.

General Comte de la Roche-Aymon, in his treatise

upon "Light Troops," published in Paris in 1856, says:

"In nearly all the European armies the equipment of the horse is not in harmony with the new tactics—with those tactics in which, during nearly all of a campaign, the cavalry remains in bivouac. Have we reflected upon the kind of saddle which, under these circumstances, would cover the horse best without incommoding him during the short periods that he is permitted to repose? Have we reflected upon the kind of saddle which, offering the least fragility, exposes the horse to the least danger of sore back? All the cuirassiers and the dragoons of Europe have saddles which they call *French saddle,* the weight of which is a load for the horse. The interior mechanism of these saddles is complicated and filled with weak bands of iron, which become deranged, bend, and sometimes break; the rider does not perceive these accidents, or he does not wish to perceive them, for fear of being left behind or of having to go on foot; he continues on, and at the end of a day's march his horse has a sore back, and in a few days is absolutely unserviceable. We may satisfy ourselves of the truth of these observations by comparing the lists of horses sent to the rear during the course of a campaign by the cuirassiers and dragoons who use the French saddle, and by the hussars with the Hungarian saddle. The number sent to the rear by the latter is infinitely less, although employed in a service much more active and severe; and it might be still less by making some slight improvements in the manner of fixing their saddle upon the horse.

"It is a long time since Marshal Saxe said there was but one kind of saddle fit for cavalry, which was the hussar saddle: this combined all advantages, lightness, solidity, and economy. It is astonishing that the system of actual war had not led to the employment of the kind of saddle in use among the Tartars, the Cossacks, the Hungarians, and, indeed, among all horsemen and nomads. This saddle has the incontestable advantage of permitting the horse to lie down and rest himself without inconvenience. If, notwithstanding the folded blanket which they place under the Hungarian saddle, this saddle will still wound the animal's back sometimes, this only proceeds from the friction occasioned by the motion of the horse and the movement of the rider upon the saddle; a friction which it will be nearly impossible to avoid, inasmuch as the saddlebow is held in its place only by a surcingle, the ends of which are united by a leathern band: these bands always relax more or less, and the saddle becomes loose. To remedy this, I propose to attach to the saddlebow itself a double girth, one end of which shall be made fast to the arch in front, and the other end to the rear of the arch upon the right side, to unite in a single girth, which would buckle to a strap attached upon the left side in the usual manner. This buckle will hold the saddle firmly in its place.

"Notwithstanding all these precautions, however, there were still some inconveniences resulting from the nature of the blanket placed under the saddle, which I sought to remedy, and I easily accomplished it. The woolen nap of the cavalry saddle blankets, not being carefully attended to, soon wears off, and leaves only the rough, coarse threads of the fabric; this absorbs the sweat from the horse, and, after it has dried and become hard, it acts like a rasp upon the withers, first taking off the hair, next the skin, and then the flesh, and, finally, the beast is rendered unserviceable.

"I sought, during the campaign of 1807, a means to remedy this evil, and I soon succeeded by a process as simple as it was cheap. I distributed among a great number of cavalry soldiers pieces of linen cloth folded double, two feet square, and previously dipped in melted tallow. This cloth was laid next to the horse's back, under the saddle blanket, and it prevented all the bad effects of the woolen blanket. No horses, after this appliance, were afflicted with sore backs. Such are the slight changes which I believe should be made in the use of the Hungarian saddle. The remainder of the equipment should remain (as it always has been) composed of a breast strap, crupper, and martingale, etc."

The improvements of the present age do not appear to have developed anything advantageous to the saddle; on the contrary, after experimenting upon numerous modifications and inventions, public sentiment has at length given the preference to the saddletree of the natives in Asia and America, which is very similar to that of the Hungarians.

SORES AND DISEASES.

If a horse be sweating at the time he is unsaddled, it is well to strap the folded saddle blanket upon his back with the surcingle, where it is allowed to remain until he is perfectly dry. This causes the back to cool gradually, and prevents scalding or swelling. Some persons are in the habit of washing their horses' backs while heated and sweating with cold water, but this is pernicious, and often produces sores. It is well enough to wash the back after it cools, but not before. After horses' backs or shoulders once become chafed and sore, it is very difficult to heal them, particularly when they are continued at work. It is better, if practicable, to stop using them for a while, and wash the bruised parts often with castile soap and water. Should it be necessary, however, to continue the animal in use, I have known very severe sores entirely healed by the free application of grease to the parts immediately after halting, and while the animal is warm and sweating. This seems to harden the skin and heal the wound even when working with the collar in contact with it. A piece of bacon rind tied upon the collar over the wound is also an excellent remedy.

In Texas, when the horseflies are numerous, they

attack animals without mercy, and where a contusion is found in the skin they deposit eggs, which speedily produce worms in great numbers. I have tried the effect of spirits of turpentine and several other remedies, but nothing seemed to have the desired effect but calomel blown into the wound, which destroyed the worms and soon effected a cure.

In the vicinity of the South Pass, upon the Humboldt River, and in some sections upon other routes to California, alkaline water is found, which is very poisonous to animals that drink it, and generates a disease known in California as "alkali." This disease first makes its appearance by swellings upon the abdomen and between the forelegs, and is attended with a cough, which ultimately destroys the lungs and kills the animal. If taken at an early stage, this disease is curable, and the following treatment is generally considered as the most efficacious. The animal is first raked, after which a large dose of grease is poured down its throat; acids are said to have the same effect, and give immediate relief. When neither of these remedies can be procured, many of the emigrants have been in the habit of mixing starch or flour in a bucket of water, and allowing the animal to drink it. It is supposed that this forms a coating over the mucous membrane, and thus defeats the action of the poison.

Animals should never be allowed to graze in the vicinity of alkaline water, as the deposits upon the grass after floods are equally deleterious with the water itself.

In seasons when the water is low in the Humboldt River, there is much less danger of the alkali, as the running water in the river then comes from pure mountain springs, and is confined to the channel; whereas, during high water, when the banks are overflowed, the salts are dissolved, making the water more impure.

For colic, a good remedy is a mixture of two tablespoonfuls of brandy and two teaspoonfuls of laudanum dissolved in a bottle of water and poured down the animal's throat. Another remedy, which has been recommended to me by an experienced officer as producing speedy relief, is a tablespoonful of chloride of lime dissolved in a bottle of water, and administered as in the other case.

RATTLESNAKE BITES.

Upon the southern routes to California rattlesnakes are often met with, but it is seldom that any person is bitten by them; yet this is a possible contingency, and it can never be amiss to have an antidote at hand.

Hartshorn applied externally to the wound, and drunk in small quantities diluted with water whenever the patient becomes faint or exhausted from the effects of the poison, is one of the most common remedies.

In the absence of all medicines, a string or ligature should at once be bound firmly above the puncture, then scarify deeply with a knife, suck out the poison, and spit out the saliva.

Andersson, in his book on Southwestern Africa, says: "In the Cape Colony the Dutch farmers resort to a cruel but apparently effective plan to counteract the bad effects of a serpent's bite. An incision having been made in the breast of a living fowl, the bitten part is applied to the wound. If the poison be very deadly, the bird soon evinces symptoms of distress, becomes drowsy, droops its head, and dies. It is replaced by a second, a third, and more if requisite. When, however, the bird no longer exhibits any of the signs just mentioned, the patient is considered out of danger. A frog similarly applied is supposed to be equally efficacious."

Haunberg, in his *Travels in South Africa,* mentions an antidote against the bite of serpents. He says: "The blood of the turtle was much cried up, which, on account of this extraordinary virtue, the inhabitants dry in the form of small scales or membranes, and carry about them when they travel in this country, which swarms with this most noxious vermin. Whenever anyone is wounded by a serpent, he takes a couple of pinches of the dried blood internally, and applies a little of it to the wound."

I was present upon one occasion when an Indian child was struck in the forefinger by a large rattlesnake. His mother, who was near at the time, seized him in her arms, and, placing the wounded finger in her mouth, sucked the poison from the puncture for some minutes, repeatedly spitting out the saliva; after which she chewed and mashed some plantain leaves and applied to the wound. Over this she sprinkled some finely powdered tobacco, and wrapped the finger up in a rag. I did not observe that the child suffered afterward the least pain or inconvenience. The immediate application of the remedies probably saved his life.

Irritation from the bite of gnats and mosquitoes, etc., may be relieved by chewing the plantain, and rubbing the spittle on the bite.

I knew of another instance near Fort Towson, in Northern Texas, where a small child was left upon the earthen floor of a cabin while its mother was washing at a spring nearby. She heard a cry of distress, and, on going to the cabin, what was her horror on seeing a rattlesnake coiled around the child's arm, and striking it repeatedly with its fangs. After killing the snake, she hurried to her nearest neighbor, procured a bottle of brandy, and returned as soon as possible; but the poison had already so operated upon the arm that it was as black as a negro's. She poured down the child's throat a huge draft of the liquor, which soon took effect, making it very drunk, and stopped the action of the poison. Although the child was relieved, it remained sick for a long time, but ultimately recovered.

A man was struck in the leg by a very large rattlesnake near Fort Belknap, Texas, in 1853. No other remedy being at hand, a small piece of indigo was pulverized, made into a poultice with water, and applied to the puncture. It seemed to draw out the poison, turning the indigo white, after which it was removed and another poultice applied. These applications were repeated until the indigo ceased to change its color. The man was then carried to the hospital at Fort Belknap, and soon recovered, and the surgeon of the post pronounced it a very satisfactory cure.

A Chickasaw woman, who was bitten upon the foot near Fort Washita by a ground rattlesnake (a very venomous species), drank a bottle of whisky and applied the indigo poultice, and when I saw her, three days afterward, she was recovering, but the flesh around the wound sloughed away.

A Delaware remedy, which is said to be efficacious, is to burn powder upon the wound, but I have never known it to be tried excepting upon a horse. In this case it was successful, or, at all events, the animal recovered.

Of all the remedies known to me, I should decidedly prefer ardent spirits. It is considered a sovereign antidote among our Western frontier settlers, and I would make use of it with great confidence. It must be taken until the patient becomes very much intoxicated, and this requires a large quantity, as the action of the poison seems to counteract its effects.

Should the fangs of the snake penetrate deep enough to reach an artery, it is probable the person would die in a short time. I imagine, however, that this does not often occur.

The following remedial measures for the treatment of the bites of poisonous reptiles are recommended by Dr. Philip Weston in the London Lancet for July 1859:

1. The application of a ligature round the limb close to the wound, between it and the heart, to arrest the return of venous blood.

2. Excision of the bitten parts, or free incision through the wounds made by the poison teeth, subsequently encouraging the bleeding by warm solutions to favor the escape of the poison from the circulation.

3. Cauterization widely round the limb of the bite with a strong solution of nitrate of silver, one drachm to the ounce, to prevent the introduction of the poison into the system by the lymphatics.

4. As soon as indications of the absorption of the poison into the circulation begin to manifest themselves, the internal administration of ammonia in aerated or soda water every quarter of an hour, to support the nervous energy and allay the distressing thirst.

"But," he continues, "there is yet wanting some remedy that shall rapidly counteract the poison introduced into the blood, and assist in expelling it from the system. The well-authenticated accounts of the success attending the internal use of arsenic in injuries arising from the bites of venomous reptiles in the East and West Indies, and also in Africa, and the well-known properties of this medicine as a powerful tonic and alternative in conditions of impaired vitality of the blood arising from the absorption of certain blood poisons, would lead me to include this agent in the treatment already mentioned. It should be administered in combination with ammonia, in full doses, frequently repeated, so as to neutralize quickly the poison circulating in the blood before it can be eliminated from the system. This could readily be accomplished by adding ten to fifteen minims of Fowler's solution to the compound spirit of ammonia, to be given every quarter of an hour in aerated or soda water, until the vomiting and the more urgent symptoms of collapse have subsided, subsequently repeating the dose at longer intervals until reaction had become fully established, and the patient relieved by copious bilious dejections."

Cedron, which is a nut that grows on the Isthmus of Panama, and which is sold by the druggists in New York, is said to be an infallible antidote to serpent bites. In the *Bullet. de l'Acad. de Méd.* for February 1858, it is stated that a man was bitten at Panama by a coral snake, the most poisonous species on the Isthmus. During the few seconds that it took him to take the cedron from his bag, he was seized with violent pains at the heart and throat; but he had scarcely chewed and swallowed a piece of the nut about the size of a small bean, when the pains ceased as by magic. He chewed a little more, and applied it externally to the wound, when the pains disappeared, and were followed by a copious evacuation of a substance like curdled milk. Many other cases are mentioned where the cedron proved an antidote.

CHAPTER V.

Bivouacs.—Tente d'Abri.—Gutta-percha Knapsack Tent.—Comanche Lodge. —Sibley Tent. —Camp Furniture. —Litters.—Rapid Traveling.—Fuel.—Making Fires.—Fires on the Prairies.—Jerking Meat.—Making Lariats.—Making Caches.—Disposition of Firearms.—Colt's Revolvers.—Gun Accidents.—Trailing.—Indian Sagacity.

BIVOUACS AND TENTS.

IN TRAVELING with pack animals it is not always convenient or practicable to transport tents, and the traveler's ingenuity is often taxed in devising the most available means for making himself comfortable and secure against winds and storms. I have often been astonished to see how soon an experienced voyager, without any resources save those provided by nature, will erect a comfortable shelter in a place where a person having no knowledge of woodcraft would never think of such a thing.

Almost all people in different parts of the world have their own peculiar methods of bivouacking.

In the severe climate of Tibet, Dr. Hooker informs us that they encamp near large rocks, which absorb the heat during the day, and give it out slowly during the night. They form, as it were, reservoirs of caloric, the influence of which is exceedingly grateful during a cold night.

In the polar regions the Eskimos live and make themselves comfortable in huts of ice or snow, and with no other combustible but oil.

The natives of Australia bury their bodies in the sand, keeping their heads only above the surface, and thus sleep warm during the chilly nights of that climate.

Fortunately for the health and comfort of travelers upon the Plains, the atmosphere is pure and dry during the greater part of the year, and it is seldom that any rain or dew is seen; neither are there marshes or ponds of stagnant water to generate putrid exhalations and poisonous malaria. The night air of the summer months is soft, exhilarating, and delightful. Persons may therefore sleep in it and inhale it with perfect impunity, and, indeed, many prefer this to breathing the confined atmosphere of a house or tent.

During the rainy season only is it necessary to seek shelter. In traveling with covered wagons one always has protection from storms, but with pack trains it becomes necessary to improvise the best substitutes for tents.

A very secure protection against storms may be constructed by planting firmly in the ground two upright poles, with forks at their tops, and crossing them with a light pole laid in the forks. A gutta-percha cloth, or sheet of canvas, or, in the absence of either of these two, blankets, may be attached by one side to the horizontal pole, the opposite edge being stretched out to the windward at an angle of about forty-five degrees to the ground, and there fastened with wooden pins, or with buckskin strings tied to the lower border of the cloth and to pegs driven firmly into the earth. This forms a shelter for three or four men, and is a good defense against winds and rains. If a fire be then made in front, the smoke will be carried away, so as not to incommode the occupants of the bivouac.

HALF-FACED CAMP.

This is called a "half-faced" camp.

Another method practiced a great deal among mountain men and Indians consists in placing several rough poles equidistant around in a half circle, and bringing the small ends together at the top, where they are bound with a thong. This forms the conical framework of the bivouac, which, when cov-

CONICAL BIVOUAC.

ered with a cloth stretched around it, makes a very good shelter, and is preferable to the half-faced camp, because the sides are covered.

When no cloths, blankets, or hides are at hand to be placed over the poles of the lodge, it may be covered with green boughs laid on compactly, so as to shed a good deal of rain, and keep out the wind in cold weather. We adopted this description of shelter in crossing the Rocky Mountains during the winter of 1857–8, and thus formed a very effectual protection against the bleak winds which sweep with great violence over those lofty and inhospitable sierras. We always selected a dense thicket for our encampment, and covered the lodges with a heavy coating of pine boughs. wattling them together as compactly as possible, and piling snow upon the outside in such a manner as to make them quite impervious to the wind. The fires were then kindled at the mouths of the lodges, and our heads and bodies were completely sheltered, while our feet were kept warm by the fires.

The French troops, while serving in the Crimea, used what they call the *tente d'abri*, or shelter tent, which seems to have been received with great favor in Europe. It is composed of two, four, or six square pieces of cloth, with buttons and buttonholes adjusted upon the edges, and is pitched by planting two upright stakes in the ground at a distance corresponding with the length of the canvas when buttoned together. The two sticks are connected by a cord passed around the top of each, drawn tight, and the ends made fast to pins driven firmly into the ground. The canvas is then laid over the rope between the sticks, spread out at an angle of about forty-five degrees, and the lower edges secured to the earth with wooden pins. This makes some defense against the weather, and was the only shelter enjoyed by the mass of the French army in the Crimea up to October 1855. For a permanent camp it is usual to excavate a shallow basement under the tent, and to bank up the earth on the outside in cold weather. It is designed that upon marches the *tente d'abri* shall be taken to pieces and carried by the soldiers.

A tent has recently been prepared by Mr. John Rider, 165 Broadway, New York, which is called the "tent knapsack." It has been examined by a board of army officers, and recommended for adoption in our military service.

This tent is somewhat similar to the *tente d'abri*, and is pitched in the same manner, but it has this advantage, that each separate piece may be converted into a waterproof knapsack.

The following extracts from the Report of the Board go to show that this tent knapsack will be useful to parties traveling on the prairies with pack trains:

> It is a piece of gutta-percha 5 feet 3 inches long, and 3 feet 8 inches wide, with double edges on one side, and brass studs and button-holes along two edges, and straps and buckles on the fourth edge; the whole weighing three pounds; two sticks, 3 feet 8 inches long by 1¼ inches in diameter, and a small cord. When used as a knapsack, the clothing is packed in a cotton bag, and the gutta-percha sheet is folded round it, lapping at the ends. The clothing is thus protected by two or three thicknesses of gutta-percha, and in this respect there is a superiority over the knapsack now used by our troops. Other advantages are, that the tent knapsack has no seams, the parts at which those in use wear out soonest; it adapts itself to the size of the contents, so that a compact and portable bundle can be made, whether the kit be entire or not; and, with the cotton bag, it forms a convenient, commodious, and du-

TENT KNAPSACK.

rable receptacle for all a soldier's clothing and necessaries.

On a scout a soldier usually carries only a blanket, overcoat, and at most a single shirt, pair of drawers, and a pair of socks, all of which can be packed in the tent knapsack in a small bundle, perfectly protected from rain, and capable of being suspended from the shoulders and carried with comfort and ease during a march.

2d. As a shelter. The studs and eyelets along two edges of the tent knapsack are for the purpose of fastening a number of them together, and thus making a sheet of larger dimensions.

A sheet formed by fastening together four knapsacks was exhibited to the Board, stretched upon a frame of wood. When used in service the sheet is to be stretched on a rope supported by two poles, or by two rifles, muskets, or carbines, and pinned down at the sides with six pins, three on each side.

The sheet of four knapsacks is 10 feet 6 inches long, and 7 feet 4 inches wide, and when pitched on a rope 4 feet 4 inches above the ground, covers a horizontal space 6 feet 6 inches wide, and 7 feet 4 inches long, which will accommodate five men, and may be made to shelter seven. The sheet can also be used on the ground, and is a great protection from dampness, and as a shawl or talma; indeed, a variety of advantageous uses to which the gutta-percha sheet may be put will suggest themselves to persons using it.

The Board is satisfied with its merits in all the uses to which it is proposed to be put, and is of opinion that the gutta-percha tent knapsack may be adopted in the military service with advantage.

The usual tenement of the prairie tribes, and of the traders, trappers, and hunters who live among them, is the Comanche lodge, which is made of eight straight peeled poles about twenty feet long, covered with hides or cloth. The lodge is pitched by connecting the smaller extremities of three of the poles with one end of a long line. The three poles are

COMANCHE LODGE.

then raised perpendicularly, and the larger extremities spread out in a tripod to the circumference of the circle that is to form the base of the lodge. The other poles are then raised, laid into the forks of the three first, and spread out equidistant upon the circle, thus forming the conical framework of the structure. Nine or ten poles are generally used in one lodge.

The long line attached to the tripod is then wound several times around the top, where the poles intersect, and the lower end made fast at the base of the lodge, thus securing the frame firmly in its position. The covering, made of buffalo hides, dressed without the hair, and cut and sewed together to fit the conical frame, is raised with a pole, spread out around the structure, and united at the edges with sharpened wooden pegs, leaving sufficient space open at the bottom for a doorway, which may be closed with a blanket spread out with two small sticks, and suspended over the opening.

The lower edge of the lodge is made fast to the ground with wooden pins. The apex is left open, with a triangular wing or flap on each side, and the windward flap constantly stretched out by means of a pole inserted into a pocket in the end of it, which causes it to draw like a sail, and thus occasions a draft from the fire built upon the ground in the center of the lodge, and makes it warm and comfortable in the coldest winter weather. Canvas makes a very good substitute for the buffalo-skin covering.

SIBLEY TENT.

A tent has been invented by Major H.H. Sibley, of the army, which is known as the "Sibley tent." It is somewhere similar to the Comanche lodge, but in place of the conical framework of poles it has but one upright standard, resting upon an iron tripod in the center. The tripod can be used to suspend cooking utensils over the fire, and, when folded up, admits the wooden standard between the legs, thereby reducing the length one half, and making it more convenient for packing and traveling.

THE SIBLEY TENT.

This tent constituted the entire shelter of the army in Utah during the winter of 1857–8, and, notwithstanding the severity of the climate in the elevated locality of Camp Scott, the troops were quite comfortable, and pleased with the tent.

In permanent camps the Sibley tent may be so pitched as to give more room by erecting a tripod upon the outside with three poles high and stout enough to admit of the tent's being suspended by ropes attached to the apex. This method dispenses with the necessity of the central upright standard.

When the weather is very cold, the tent may be made warmer by excavating a basement about three feet deep, which also gives a wall to the tent, making it more roomy.

The tent used in the army will shelter comfortably twelve men.

Captain G. Rhodes, of the English army, in his recent work upon tents and tent life, has given a description of most of the tents used in the different armies in Europe, but, in my judgment, none of them, in point of convenience, comfort, and economy, will compare with the Sibley tent for campaigning in cold weather. One of its most important features, that of admitting of a fire within it and of causing a draft by the disposition of the wings, is not, that I am aware, possessed by any other tent. Moreover, it is exempt from the objections that are urged against some other tents on account of insalubrity from want of top ventilation to carry off the impure air during the night.

CAMP FURNITURE.

The accompanying illustrations present some convenient articles of portable camp furniture.

Camp Chair No. 1 is of oak or other hard wood. Fig. 1 represents it opened for us; in Fig. 2 it is closed for transportation. *A* is a stout canvas, forming the back and seat; *b, b, b* are iron butt hinges; *c, c* are leather straps, one inch and a quarter wide, forming the arms; *d* is an iron rod, with nut and screw at one end.

Camp Chair No. 2 is made of sticks tied together with thongs of buckskin or raw hide.

Camp Chair No. 3 is a very comfortable seat, made of a barrel, the part forming the seat being filled with grass.

Camp Table. Fig. 1 represents the table folded for transportation; in Fig. 2 it is spread out for use. *A* is the top of the table; *a, a* are side boards, and *c, c* are end boards, turning on butt hinges, *b,b,b.*

Field Cots. In No. 1, *A* represents the cot put up for use; *B*, the cot folded for transportation. The legs turn upon iron bolts running through the head and foot boards; they are then placed upon the canvas, and the whole is rolled up around the side pieces. In No. 2 the upper figure represents the cot put up for use; the lower shows it folded for transportation. *A* is a stout canvas; *b, b* are iron butt hinges; *c, c,* the legs; *d, d,* leather straps with buckles, which hold the legs firm; *f, f,* ends, which fold

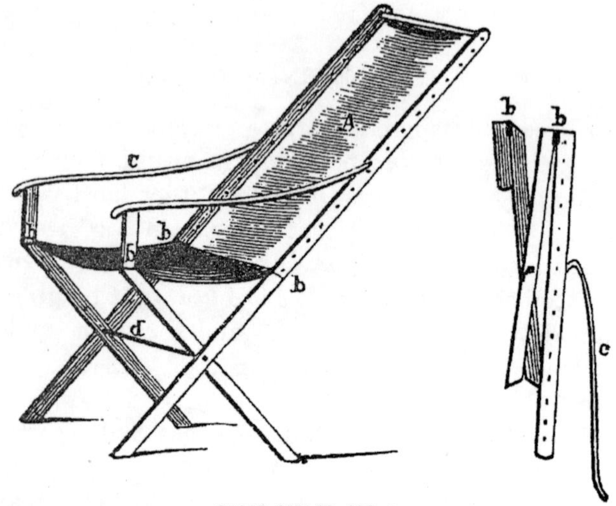

CAMP CHAIR. NO. 1.

CAMP CHAIRS. NOS. 2 AND 3.

Fig. 1.

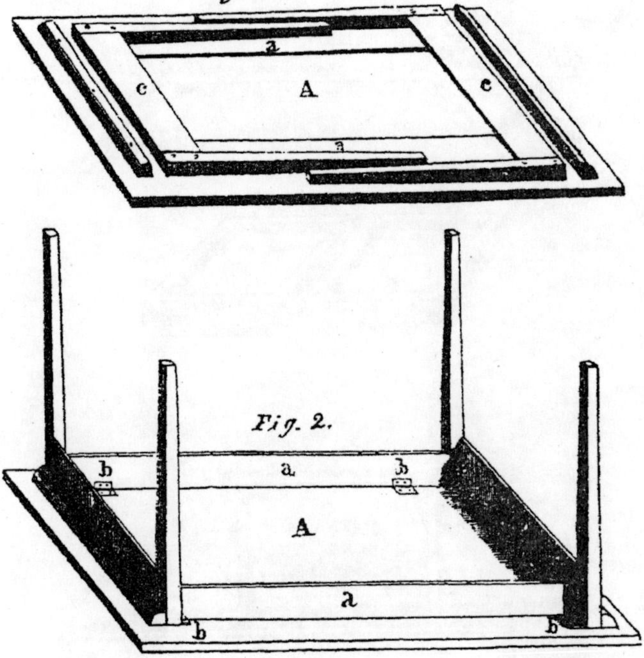

CAMP TABLE

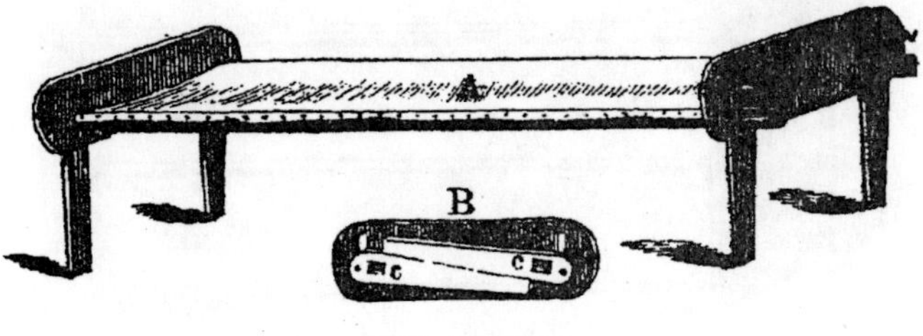

FIELD COT. NO. 1.

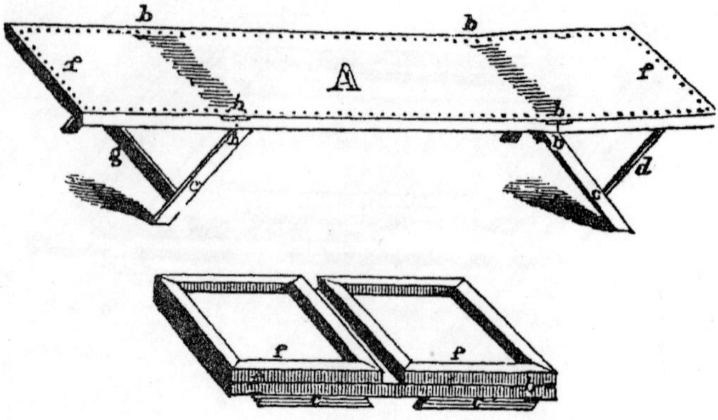

FIELD COT. NO. 2.

CAMP BUREAU.

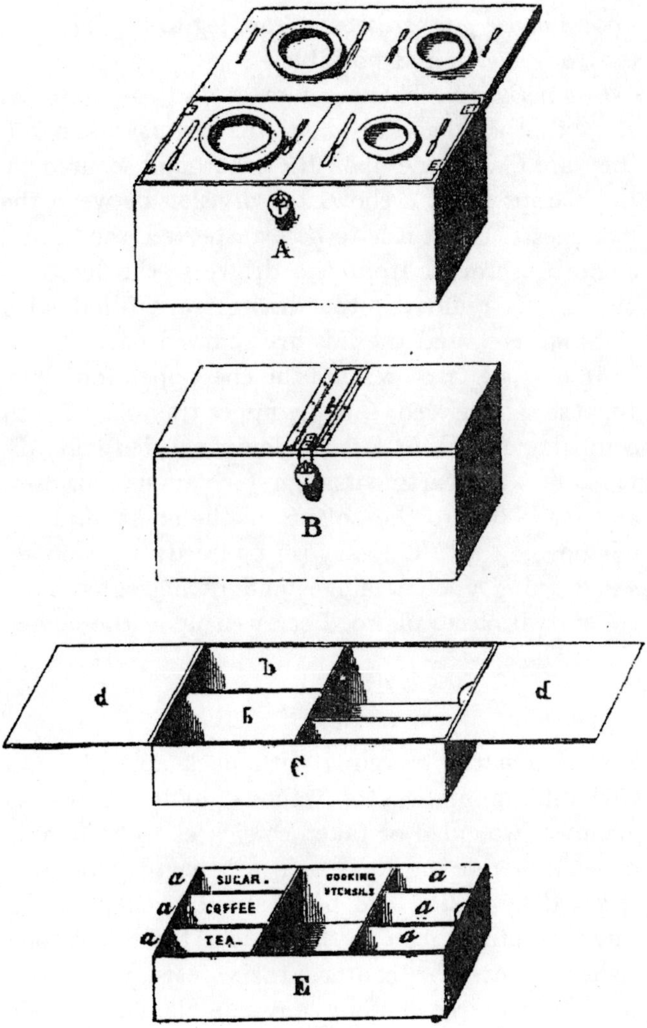

MESS CHEST.

upon hinges; *g, g,* crossbars from leg to leg. This cot is strong, light, and portable.

Camp Bureau. This cut represents two chests, *A, A,* with their handles, *a, a;* the covers taken off, they are placed one upon the other, and secured by the clamps *B, B; d* shows the division between the two chests. When it is to be transported, the knobs, *c,* are unscrewed from the drawers, the looking-glass, *f,* is removed, the drawers are filled with clothing, etc., and the lids are screwed on.

Mess Chest. A represents the chest open for table; *B* is the same closed; *C* is the upper tray of tin, with compartments, *b, b; E* is the lower wooden tray, divided into compartments, *a, a,* for various purposes, and made fast to the bottom of the chest; *d, d* are lids opening with hinges; *f* (in figure B) is a wooden leg, turning upon a hinge, and fitting snugly between two pieces of wood screwed upon the cover.

LITTERS.

Should a party traveling with pack animals, and without ambulances or wagons, have one of its members wounded or taken so sick as to be unable to walk or ride on horseback, a litter may be constructed by taking two poles about twenty feet in length, uniting them by two sticks three feet long lashed across the center at six feet apart, and stretching a piece of stout canvas, a blanket, or hide between them to form the bed. Two steady horses

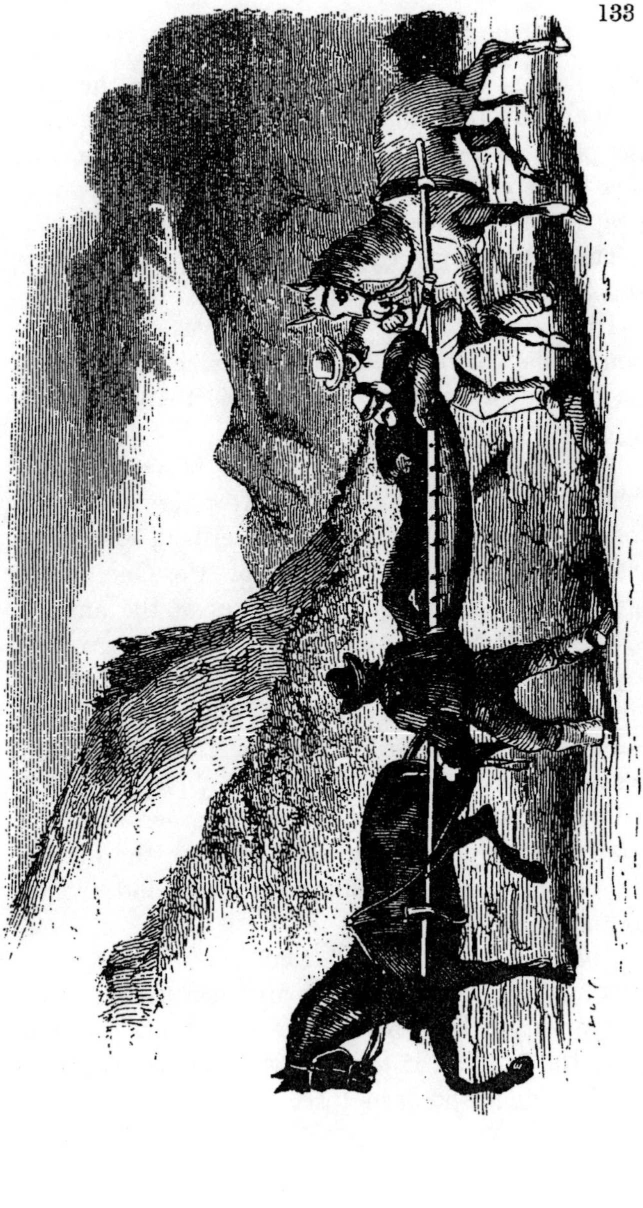

HORSE LITTER.

or mules are then selected, placed between the poles in the front and rear of the litter, and the ends of the poles made fast to the sides of the animals, either by attachment to the stirrups or to the ends of straps secured over their backs.

The patient may then be placed upon the litter, and is ready for the march.

The elasticity of the long poles gives an easy motion to the conveyance, and makes this method of locomotion much more comfortable than might be supposed.

The prairie Indians have a way of transporting their sick and children upon a litter very similar in construction to the one just described, excepting that one animal is used instead of two. One end of the litter is made fast to the sides of the animal, while the other end is left to trail upon the ground. A projection is raised for the feet to rest against and prevent the patient from sliding down. Instead of canvas, the Indians sometimes lash a large willow basket across the poles, in which they place the person to be transported. The animals harnessed to the litter must be carefully conducted upon the march, and caution used in passing over rough and broken ground.

A very convenient and comfortable method of packing a sick or wounded man when there are no animals disposable, and which is sometimes resorted to by the Indians, is to take two small poles about ten feet long, and lash three crosspieces to them, one in the center, and the other two about eighteen inches from the ends. A blanket or hide is then secured firmly to this frame, and the patient placed upon it under the center crosspiece, which prevents him from falling out. Two men act as carriers, walking between the ends of the long poles. The patient may be protected against the rain or sun by bending small willows over the frame, and covering them with a cloth.

HAND LITTER.

RAPID TRAVELING.

Small parties with good animals, light vehicles, and little lading, may traverse the Plains rapidly and comfortably, if the following injunctions be observed.

The day's drive should commence as soon as it is light, and, where the road is good, the animals kept upon a slow trot for about three hours, then immediately turned out upon the best grass that can be found for two hours, thus giving time for grazing and breakfast. After which another drive of about three hours may be made, making the noon halt about three hours, when the animals are again harnessed, and the journey continued until night.

In passing through a country infested by hostile Indians, the evening drive should be prolonged until an hour or two after dark, turning off at a point where the ground is hard, going about half a mile from the road, and encamping without fires, in low ground, where the Indians will find it difficult to track or see the party.

These frequent halts serve to rest and recruit the animals so that they will, without injury, make from thirty to forty miles a day for a long time. This, however, can only be done with very light loads and vehicles, such, for example, as an ambulance with four mules, only three or four persons, and a small amount of luggage.

FUEL AND FIRE.

There are long distances upon some of the routes to California where no other fuel is found but the dried dung of the buffalo, called by the mountaineers "chips," and by the French *bois de vache,* the *argul* of the Tartary deserts. It burns well when perfectly dry, answers a good purpose for cooking, and some men even prefer it to wood. As it will not burn when wet, it is well, in a country where no other fuel can be had, when it threatens to rain, for the traveler to collect a supply before the rain sets in, and carry it in wagons to the camp. When dry, the chips are easily lighted.

A great saving in fuel may be made by digging a trench about two feet long by eight inches in width and depth; the fires are made in the bottom of the trench, and the cooking utensils placed upon the top, where they receive all the heat. This plan is especially recommended for windy weather, and it is convenient at all times. The wood should be cut short, and split into small pieces.

It is highly important that travelers should know the different methods that may be resorted to for kindling fires upon a march.

The most simple and most expeditious of these is by using the lucifer matches; but, unless they are kept in well-corked bottles, they are liable to become wet, and will then fail to ignite.

The most of those found in the shops easily imbibe dampness, and are of but little use in the prairies. Those marked "Van Duser, New York," and put up in flat rectangular boxes, are the best I have met with, and were the only ones I saw which were not affected by the humid climate of Mexico. Wax lucifers are better than wooden, as they are impervious to moisture.

I have seen an Indian start a fire with flint and steel after others have failed to do it with matches. This was during a heavy rain, when almost all available fuel had become wet. On such occasions dry fuel may generally be obtained under logs, rocks, or leaning trees.

The inner bark of some dry trees, cedar for instance, is excellent to kindle a fire. The bark is rubbed in the hand until the fibers are made fine and loose, when it takes fire easily; dry grass or leaves are also good. After a sufficient quantity of small kindling fuel has been collected, a moistened rag is rubbed with powder, and a spark struck into it with a flint and steel, which will ignite it; this is then placed in the center of the loose nest of inflammable material, and whirled around in the air until it bursts out into a flame. When it is raining, the blaze should be laid upon the dryest spot that can be found, a blanket held over it to keep off the water, and it is fed with very small bits of dry wood and shavings until it has gained sufficient strength to burn the larger damp wood. When no dry place can be found, the fire may be started in a kettle or frying pan, and afterward transferred to the ground.

Should there be no other means of starting a fire, it can always be made with a gun or pistol, by placing upon the ground a rag saturated with damp powder, and a little dry powder sprinkled over it. The gun or pistol is then (uncharged) placed with the cone directly over and near the rag, and a cap exploded, which will invariably ignite it. Another method is by placing about one-fourth of a charge of powder into a gun, pushing a rag down loosely upon it, and firing it out with the muzzle down near the ground, which ignites the rag.

The most difficult of all methods of making a fire, but one that is practiced by some of the Western Indians, is by friction between two pieces of wood. I had often heard of this process, but never gave credit to its practicability until I saw the experiment successfully tried. It was done in the following manner: Two dried stalks of the Mexican soap plant, about three-fourths of an inch in diameter, were selected, and one of them made flat on one side; near the edge of this flat surface a very small indentation was made to receive the end of the other stick, and a groove cut from this down the side. The other stick is cut with a rounded end, and placed upright upon the first. One man then holds the horizontal piece upon the ground, while another takes the vertical stick between the palms of his hands, and turns it back and forth as rapidly as possible, at the same time pressing forcibly down upon it. The point of the upright stick wears away the indentation into a fine powder, which runs off to the ground in the groove that has been cut; after a time it begins to smoke, and by continued friction it will at length take fire.

This is an operation that is difficult, and requires practice; but if a drill stick is used with a cord placed around the center of the upright stick, it can be turned much more rapidly than with the hands, and the fire produced more readily. The upright stick may be of any hard, dry wood, but the lower horizontal stick must be of a soft, inflammable nature, such as pine, cottonwood, or black walnut, and it must be perfectly dry. The Indians work the sticks with the palms of the hands, holding the lower piece between the feet; but it is better to have a man to hold the lower piece while another man works the drill bow.

Inexperienced travelers are very liable, in kindling fires at their camp, to ignite the grass around them. Great caution should be taken to guard against the occurrence of such accidents, as they might prove exceedingly disastrous. We were very near having our entire train of wagons and supplies destroyed, upon one occasion, by the carelessness of one of our party in setting fire to the grass, and it was only by the most strenuous and well-timed efforts of two hundred men in setting counter fires, and burning around the train, that it was saved.

When the grass is dry it will take fire like powder, and if thick and tall, with a brisk wind, the flames run like a racehorse, sweeping everything before them. A lighted match, or the ashes from a cigar or pipe, thrown carelessly into the dry grass, sometimes sets it on fire; but the greatest danger lies in kindling campfires.

To prevent accidents of this kind, before kindling the fire a space should be cleared away sufficient to embrace the limits of the flame, and all combustibles removed therefrom, and while the fire is being made men should be stationed around with blankets ready to put it out if it takes the grass.

When a fire is approaching, and escape from its track is impossible, it may be repelled in the following manner: The train and animals are parked compactly together; then several men, provided with blankets, set fire to the grass on the lee side, burning it away gradually from the train, and extinguishing it on the side next the train. This can easily be done, and the fire controlled with the blankets, or with dry sand thrown upon it, until an area large enough to give room for the train has been burned clear. Now the train moves on to this ground of safety, and the fire passes by harmless.

JERKING MEAT.

So pure is the atmosphere in the interior of our continent that fresh meat may be cured, or *jerked,* as it is termed in the language of the prairies, by cutting it into strips about an inch thick, and hanging it in the sun, where in a few days it will dry so well that it may be packed in sacks, and transported over long journeys without putrefying.

When there is not time to jerk the meat by the slow process described, it may be done in a few hours by building an open framework of small sticks about two feet above the ground, placing the strips of meat upon the top of it, and keeping up a slow fire beneath, which dries the meat rapidly.

The jerking process may be done upon the march without any loss of time by stretching lines from front to rear upon the outside of loaded wagons, and suspending the meat upon them, where it is allowed to remain until sufficiently cured to be packed away. Salt is never used in this process, and is not required, as the meat, if kept dry, rarely putrefies.

If travelers have ample transportation, it will be a wise precaution, in passing through the buffalo range, to lay in a supply of jerked meat for future exigences.

LARIATS.

It frequently happens upon long journeys that the lariat ropes wear out or are lost, and if there were no means of replacing them great inconvenience might result therefrom. A very good substitute may be made by taking the green hide of a buffalo, horse, mule, or ox, stretching it upon the ground, and pinning it down by the edges. After it has been well stretched, a circle is described with a piece of charcoal, embracing as much of the skin as practicable, and a strip about an inch wide cut from the outer edge of sufficient length to form the lariat. The strip is then wrapped around between two trees or stakes, drawn tight, and left to dry, after which it is subjected to a process of friction until it becomes pliable, when it is ready for use; this lariat answers well so long as it is kept dry, but after it has been wet and dried again it becomes very hard and unyielding. This, however, may be obviated by boiling it in oil or grease until thoroughly saturated, after which it remains pliable.

The Indians make very good lariat ropes of dressed buffalo or buckskins cut into narrow strips and braided; these, when oiled, slip much more freely than the hemp or cotton ropes, and are better for lassoing animals, but they are not as suitable for picketing as those made of other material, because the wolves will eat them, and thus set free the animals to which they are attached.

CACHES.

It not unfrequently happens that travelers are compelled, for want of transportation, to abandon a portion of their luggage, and if it is exposed to the keen scrutiny of the thieving savages who often follow the trail of a party, and hunt over old camps for such things as may be left, it will be likely to be appropriated by them. Such contingencies have given rise to a method of secreting articles called by the old French Canadian voyagers "caching."

The proper places for making caches are in loose sandy soils, where the earth is dry and easily excavated. Near the bank of a river is the most convenient for this purpose, as the earth taken out can be thrown into the water, leaving no trace behind.

When the spot has been chosen, the turf is carefully cut and laid aside, after which a hole is dug in the shape of an egg, and of sufficient dimensions to contain the articles to be secreted, and the earth, as it is taken out, thrown upon a cloth or blanket, and carried to a stream or ravine, where it can be disposed of, being careful not to scatter any upon the ground near the cache. The hole is then lined with bushes or dry grass, the articles placed within, covered with grass, the hole filled up with earth, and the sods carefully placed back in their original position, and everything that would be likely to attract an Indian's attention removed from the locality. If an India-rubber or gutta-percha cloth is disposable, it should be used to envelop the articles in the cache.

Another plan of making a cache is to dig the hole inside a tent, and occupy the tent for some days after the goods are deposited. This effaces the marks of excavation.

The mountain traders were formerly in the habit of building fires over their caches, but the Indians have become so familiar with this practice that I should think it no longer safe.

Another method of caching which is sometimes resorted to is to place the articles in the top of an evergreen tree, such as the pine, hemlock, or spruce. The thick boughs are so arranged around the packages that they cannot be seen from beneath, and they are tied to a limb to prevent them from being blown out by the wind. This will only answer for such articles as will not become injured by the weather.

Caves or holes in the rocks that are protected from the rains are also secure deposits for caching goods, but in every case care must be taken to obliterate all tracks or other indications of men having been near them. These caches will be more secure when made at some distance from roads or trails, and in places where Indians would not be likely to pass.

To find a cache again, the bearing and distance from the center of it to some prominent object, such as a mound, rock, or tree, should be carefully determined and recorded, so that anyone, on returning to the spot, would have no difficulty in ascertaining its position.

DISPOSITION OF FIREARMS.

The mountaineers and trappers exercise a very wise precaution, on lying down for the night, by placing their arms and ammunition by their sides, where they can be seized at a moment's notice. This rule is never departed from, and they are therefore seldom liable to be surprised. In Parkyns's "Abyssinia," I find the following remarks upon this subject:

"When getting sleepy, you return your rifle between your legs, roll over, and go to sleep. Some people may think this is a queer place for a rifle; but, on the contrary, it is the position of all others where utility and comfort are most combined. The butt rests on the arm, and serves as a pillow for the head; the muzzle points between the knees, and the arms encircle the lock and breech, so that you have a smooth pillow, and are always prepared to start up armed at a moment's notice."

I have never made the experiment of sleeping in this way, but I should imagine that a gun stock would make rather a hard pillow.

Many of our experienced frontier officers prefer carrying their pistols in a belt at their sides to placing them in holsters attached to the saddle, as in the former case they are always at hand when they are dismounted; whereas, by the other plan, they become useless when a man is unhorsed, unless he has time to remove them from the saddle, which, during the excitement of an action, would seldom be the case.

Notwithstanding Colt's army- and navy-sized revolvers have been in use for a long time in our army, officers are by no means of one mind as to their relative merits for frontier service. The navy pistol, being more light and portable, is more convenient for the belt, but it is very questionable in my mind whether these qualities counterbalance the advantages derived from the greater weight of powder and lead that can be fired from the larger pistol, and the consequent increased projectile force.

This point is illustrated by an incident which fell under my own observation. In passing near the "Medicine-Bow Butte" during the spring of 1858, I most unexpectedly encountered and fired at a full-grown grizzly bear; but, as my horse had become somewhat blown by a previous gallop, his breathing so much disturbed my aim that I missed the animal at the short distance of about fifty yards, and he ran off. Fearful, if I stopped to reload my rifle, the bear would make his escape, I resolved to drive him back to the advanced guard of our escort, which I could see approaching in the distance; this I succeeded in doing, when several mounted men, armed with the navy revolvers, set off in pursuit. They approached within a few paces, and discharged ten or twelve shots, the most of which entered the animal, but he still kept on, and his progress did not seem materially impeded by the wounds. After these men had exhausted their charges, another man rode up armed with the army revolver, and fired two shots, which brought the stalwart beast to the ground.

Upon skinning him and making an examination of the wounds, it was discovered that none of the balls from the small pistols had, after passing through his thick and tough hide, penetrated deeper than about an inch into the flesh, but that the two balls from the large pistol had gone into the vitals and killed him. This test was to my mind a decisive one as to the relative efficiency of the two arms for frontier service, and I resolved thenceforth to carry the larger size.

Several different methods are practiced in slinging and carrying firearms upon horseback. The shoulder strap, with a swivel to hook into a ring behind the guard, with the muzzle resting downward in a leather cup attached by a strap to the same staple as the stirrup leather, is a very handy method for cavalry soldiers to sling their carbines; but, the gun being reversed, the jolting caused by the motion of the horse tends to move the charge and shake the powder out of the cone, which renders it liable to burst the gun and to miss fire.

An invention of the Namaquas, in Africa, described by Galton in his *Art of Travel,* is as follows:

"Sew a bag of canvas, leather, or hide, of such bigness as to admit the butt of the gun pretty freely. The straps that support it buckle through a ring in the pommel, and the thongs by which its slope is adjusted fasten round the girth below. The exact adjustments may not be hit upon by an unpracticed person for some little time, but, when they

THE GRIZZLY.

are once ascertained, the straps need never be shifted. The gun is perfectly safe, and never comes below the arm-pit, even in taking a drop leap; it is pulled out in an instant by bringing the elbow in front of the gun and close to the side, so as to throw the gun to the outside of the arm; then, lowering the hand, the gun is caught up. It is a bungling way to take out the gun while its barrel lies between the arm and the body. Any sized gun can be carried in this fashion. It offers no obstacle to mounting or dismounting."

This may be a convenient way of carrying the gun; I have never tried it. Of all methods I have used, I prefer, for hunting, a piece of leather about twelve inches by four, with a hole cut in each end; one of the ends is placed over the pommel of the saddle, and with a buckskin string made fast to it, where it remains a permanent fixture. When the rider is mounted, he places his gun across the strap upon the saddle, and carries the loose end forward over the pommel, the gun resting horizontally across his legs. It will now only be necessary occasionally to steady the gun with the hand. After a little practice the rider will be able to control it with his knees, and it will be found a very easy and convenient method of carrying it. When required for use, it is taken out in an instant by simply raising it with the hand, when the loose end of the strap comes off the pommel.

The chief causes of accidents from the use of firearms arise from carelessness, and I have always observed that those persons who are most familiar with their use are invariably the most careful. Many accidents have happened from carrying guns with the cock down upon the cap. When in this position, a blow upon the cock, and sometimes the concussion produced by the falling of the gun, will explode the cap; and, occasionally, when the cock catches a twig, or in the clothes, and lifts it from the cap, it will explode. With a gun at half cock there is but little danger of such accidents; for, when the cock is drawn back, it either comes to the full cock, and remains, or it returns to the half cock, but does not go down upon the cone. Another source of very many sad and fatal accidents resulting from the most stupid and culpable carelessness is in persons standing before the muzzles of guns and attempting to pull them out of wagons, or to draw them through a fence or brush in the same position. If the cock encounters an obstacle in its passage, it will, of course, be drawn back and fall upon the cap. These accidents are of frequent occurrence, and the cause is well understood by all, yet men continue to disregard it, and their lives pay the penalty of their indiscretion. It is a wise maxim, which applies with especial force in campaigning on the prairies, *Always look to your gun, but never let your gun look at you.*

An equally important maxim might be added to this: *Never to point your gun at another, whether charged or uncharged, and never allow another to point his gun at you.* Young men, before they become accustomed to the use of arms, are very apt to be careless, and a large percentage of gun accidents may be traced to this cause. That finished sportsman and wonderful shot, my friend Captain Martin Scott, than whom a more gallant soldier never fought a battle, was the most careful man with firearms I ever knew, and up to the time he received his death wound upon the bloody field of Molino del Rey he never ceased his cautionary advice to young officers upon this subject. His extended experience and intimate acquaintance with the use of arms had fully impressed him with its importance, and no man ever lived whose opinions upon this subject should carry greater weight. As incomprehensible as it may appear to persons accustomed to the use of firearms, recruits are very prone, before they have been drilled at target practice with ball cartridges, to place the ball below the powder in the piece. Officers conducting detachments through the Indian country should therefore give their special attention to this, and require the recruits to tear the cartridge and pour all the powder into the piece before the ball is inserted.

As accidents often occur in camp from the accidental discharge of firearms that have capped, I would recommend that the arms be continually kept loaded in campaigning, but the caps not placed upon the cones until they are required for firing.

This will cause but little delay in an action, and will conduce much to security from accidents.

When loaded firearms have been exposed for any considerable time to a moist atmosphere, they should be discharged, or the cartridges drawn, and the arms thoroughly cleaned, dried, and oiled. Too much attention cannot be given in keeping arms in perfect firing order.

TRAILING.

I know of nothing in the woodman's education of so much importance, or so difficult to acquire, as the art of trailing or tracking men and animals. To become an adept in this art requires the constant practice of years, and with some men a lifetime does not suffice to learn it.

Almost all the Indians whom I have met with are proficient in this species of knowledge, the faculty for acquiring which appears to be innate with them. Exigencies of woodland and prairie life stimulate the savage from childhood to develop faculties so important in the arts of war and of the chase.

I have seen very few white men who were good trailers, and practice did not seem very materially to improve their faculties in this regard; they have not the same acute perceptions for these things as the Indian or the Mexican. It is not apprehended that this difficult branch of woodcraft can be taught from books, as it pertains almost exclusively to the school of practice, yet I will give some facts relating to the habits of the Indians that will facilitate its acquirement.

A party of Indians, for example, starting out upon a war excursion, leave their families behind, and never transport their lodges; whereas, when they move with their families, they carry their lodges and other effects. If, therefore, an Indian trail is discovered with the marks of the lodgepoles upon it, it has certainly not been made by a war party; but if the track do not show the trace of lodgepoles, it will be equally certain that a war or hunting party has passed that way, and if it is not desired to come in conflict with them, their direction may be avoided. Mustangs or wild horses, when moving from place to place, leave a trail which is sometimes difficult to distinguish from that made by a mounted party of Indians, especially if the mustangs do not stop to graze. This may be determined by following upon the trail until some dung is found, and if this should lie in a single pile, it is a sure indication that a herd of mustangs has passed, as they always stop to relieve themselves, while a party of Indians would keep their horses in motion, and the ordure would be scattered along the road. If the trail pass through woodland, the mustangs will occasionally go under the limbs of trees too low to admit the passage of a man on horseback.

An Indian, on coming to a trail, will generally tell at a glance its age, by what particular tribe it was made, the number of the party, and many other things connected with it astounding to the uninitiated.

I remember, upon one occasion, as I was riding with a Delaware upon the prairies, we crossed the trail of a large party of Indians traveling with lodges. The tracks appeared to me quite fresh, and I remarked to the Indian that we must be near the party. "Oh no," said he, "the trail was made two days before, in the morning," at the same time pointing with his finger to where the sun would be at about 8 o'clock. Then, seeing that my curiosity was excited to know by what means he arrived at this conclusion, he called my attention to the fact that there had been no dew for the last two nights, but that on the previous morning it had been heavy. He then pointed out to me some spears of grass that had been pressed down into the earth by the horses' hoofs, upon which the sand still adhered, having dried on, thus clearly showing that the grass was wet when the tracks were made.

At another time, as I was traveling with the same Indian, I discovered upon the ground what I took to be a bear track, with a distinctly marked impression of the heel and all the toes. I immediately called the Indian's attention to it, at the same time flattering myself that I had made quite an important discovery, which had escaped his observation. The fellow remarked with a smile, "Oh no, captain, may be so he not bear track." He then pointed with his gun rod to some spears of grass that grew near the impression, but I did not comprehend the mystery until he dismounted and explained to me that, when the wind was blowing, the spears of grass would be bent over toward the ground, and the oscillating motion thereby produced would scoop out the loose sand into the shape I have described. The truth of this explanation was apparent, yet it occurred to me that its solution would have baffled the wits of most white men.

Fresh tracks generally show moisture where the earth has been turned up, but after a short exposure to the sun they become dry. If the tracks be very recent, the sand may sometimes, where it is very loose and dry, be seen running back into the tracks, and by following them to a place where they cross water, the earth will be wet for some distance after they leave it. The droppings of the dung from animals are also good indications of the age of a trail. It is well to remember whether there have been any rains within a few days, as the age of a trail may sometimes be conjectured in this way. It is very easy to tell whether tracks have been made before or after a rain, as the water washes off all the sharp edges.

It is not a difficult matter to distinguish the tracks of American horses from those of Indian horses, as the latter are never shod; moreover, they are much smaller.

In trailing horses, there will be no trouble while

the ground is soft, as the impressions they leave will then be deep and distinct; but when they pass over hard or rocky ground, it is sometimes a very slow and troublesome process to follow them. Where there is grass, the trace can be seen for a considerable time, as the grass will be trodden down and bent in the direction the party has moved; should the grass have returned to its upright position, the trail can often be distinguished by standing upon it and looking ahead for some distance in the direction it has been pursuing; the grass that has been turned over will show a different shade of green from that around it, and this often marks a trail for a long time.

Should all traces of the track be obliterated in certain localities, it is customary with the Indians to follow on in the direction it has been pursuing for a time, and it is quite probable that in some place where the ground is more favorable it will show itself again. Should the trail not be recovered in this way, they search for a place where the earth is soft, and make a careful examination, embracing the entire area where it is likely to run.

Indians who find themselves pursued and wish to escape, scatter as much as possible, with an understanding that they are to meet again at some point in advance, so that, if the pursuing party follows any one of the tracks, it will invariably lead to the place of rendezvous. If, for example, the trail points in the direction of a mountain pass, or toward any other place which affords the only passage through a particular section of country, it would not be worthwhile to spend much time in hunting it, as it would probably be regained at the pass.

As it is important in trailing Indians to know at what gaits they are traveling, and as the appearance of the tracks of horses are not familiar to all, I have in the following cut represented the prints made by the hoofs at the ordinary speed of the walk, trot, and gallop, so that persons, in following the trail of Indians, may form an idea as to the probability of overtaking them, and regulate their movements accordingly.

In traversing a district of unknown country where there are no prominent landmarks, and with the view of returning to the point of departure, a pocket compass should always be carried, and attached by a string to a buttonhole of the coat, to prevent its being lost or mislaid; and on starting out, as well as frequently during the trip, to take the bearing, and examine the appearance of the country when facing toward the starting point, as a landscape presents a very different aspect when viewing it from opposite directions. There are few white men who can retrace their steps for any great distance unless they take the above precautions in passing over an unknown country for the first time; but with the Indians it is different; the sense of locality seems to be innate with them, and they do not require the aid of the magnetic needle to guide them.

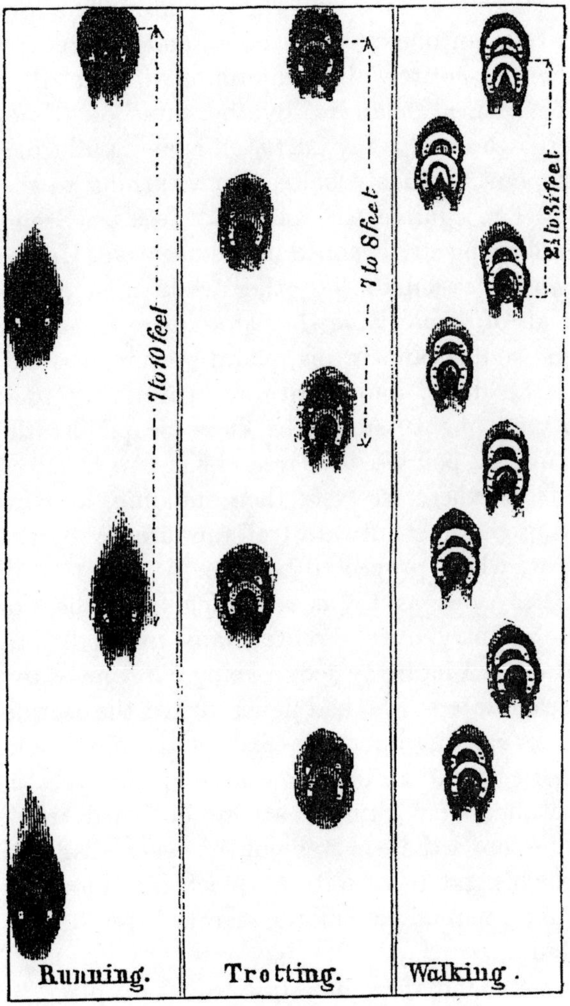

HORSE TRACKS AT ORDINARY SPEED.

Upon a certain occasion, when I had made a long march over an unexplored section, and was returning upon an entirely different route without either road or trail, a Delaware, by the name of "Black Beaver," who was in my party, on arriving at a particular point, suddenly halted, and, turning to me, asked if I recognized the country before us. Seeing no familiar objects, I replied in the negative. He put the same question to the other white men of the party, all of whom gave the same answers, whereupon he smiled, and in his quaint vernacular said, "Injun he don't know nothing. Injun big fool. White man mighty smart; he know heap." At the same time he pointed to a tree about two hundred yards from where we were then standing, and informed us that our outward trail ran directly by the side of it, which proved to be true.

Another time, as I was returning from the Comanche country over a route many miles distant from the one I had traveled in going out, one of my Delaware hunters, who had never visited the section before, on arriving upon the crest of an eminence in the prairie, pointed out to me a clump of trees in the distance, remarking that our outward track would be found there. I was not, however, disposed to credit his statement until we reached the locality and found the road passing the identical spot he had indicated.

This same Indian would start from any place to which he had gone by a sinuous route, through an unknown country, and keep a direct bearing back to the place of departure; and he assured me that he has never, even during the most cloudy or foggy weather, or in the darkest nights, lost the points of compass. There are very few white men who are endowed with these wonderful faculties, and those few are only rendered proficient by matured experience.

I have known several men, after they had become lost in the prairies, to wander about for days without exercising the least judgment, and finally exhibiting a state of mental aberration almost upon the verge of lunacy. Instead of reasoning upon their situation, they exhaust themselves running ahead at their utmost speed without any regard to direction. When a person is satisfied that he has lost his way, he should stop and reflect upon the course he has been traveling, the time that has elapsed since he left his camp, and the probable distance that he is from it; and if he is unable to retrace his steps, he should keep as nearly in the direction of them as possible; and if he has a compass, this will be an easy matter; but, above all, he should guard against following his own track around in a circle with the idea that he is in a beaten trace.

When he is traveling with a train of wagons which leaves a plain trail, he can make the distance he has traveled from camp the radius of a circle in which to ride around, and before the circle is described he will strike the trail. If the person has no compass, it is always well to make an observation, and to remember the direction of the wind at the time of departure from camp; and as this would not generally change during the day, it would afford a means of keeping the points of the compass.

In the night Ursa Major (the Great Bear) is not only useful to find the north star, but its position, when the pointers will be vertical in the heavens, may be estimated with sufficient accuracy to determine the north even when the north star can not be seen. In tropical latitudes, the zodiacal stars, such as Orion and Antares, give the east and west bearing, and the Southern Cross the north and south when Polaris and the Great Bear can not be seen.

It is said that the moss upon the firs and other trees in Europe gives a certain indication of the points of compass in a forest country, the greatest amount accumulating upon the north side of the trees. But I have often observed the trees in our own forests, and have not been able to form any positive conclusions in this way.

CHAPTER VI.

Guides and Hunters. —Delawares and Shawnees. —Khebirs. —Black Beaver. —Anecdotes. —Domestic Troubles. —Lodges. —Similarity of Prairie Tribes to the Arabs. —Method of making War. —Tracking and pursuing Indians. —Method of attacking them. —Telegraphing by Smokes.

DELAWARES AND SHAWNEES.

It is highly important that parties making expeditions through an unexplored country should secure the services of the best guides and hunters, and I know of none who are superior to the Delawares and Shawnee Indians. They have been with me upon several different occasions, and I have invariably found them intelligent, brave, reliable, and in every respect well qualified to fill their positions. They are endowed with those keen and wonderful powers in woodcraft which can only be acquired by instinct, practice, and necessity, and which are possessed by no other people that I have heard of, unless it be the khebirs or guides who escort the caravans across the great desert of Sahara.

General E. Dumas, in his treatise upon the "Great Desert," published in Paris, 1856, in speaking of these guides, says:

The khebir is always a man of intelligence, of tried probity, bravery, and skill. He knows how to determine his position from the appearance of the stars; by the experience of other journeys he has learned all about the roads, wells, and pastures; the dangers of certain passes, and the means of avoiding them; all the chiefs whose territories it is necessary to pass through; the salubrity of the different localities; the remedies against diseases; the treatment of fractures, and the antidotes to the venom of snakes and scorpions.

In these vast solitudes, where nothing seems to indicate the route, where the wind covers up all traces of the track with sand, the khebir has a thousand ways of directing himself in the right course. In the night, when there are no stars in sight, by the simple inspection of a handful of grass, which he examines with his fingers, which he smells and tastes, he informs himself of his locale without ever being lost or wandering.

I saw with astonishment that our conductor, although he had but one eye, and that defective, recognized perfectly the route; and Leon, the African, states that the conductor of his caravan became blind upon the journey from ophthalmia, yet by feeling the grass and sand he could tell when we were approaching an inhabited place.

Our guide had all the qualities which make a good khebir. He was young, large, and strong; he was a master of arms; his eye commanded respect, and his speech won the heart. But if in the tent he was affable and winning, once en route he spoke only when it was necessary, and never smiled.

The Delawares are but a minute remnant of the great Algonquin family, whose early traditions declare them to be the parent stock from which the other numerous branches of the Algonquin tribes originated. And they are the same people whom the first white settlers found so numerous upon the banks of the Delaware.

When William Penn held his council with the Delawares upon the ground where the city of Philadelphia now stands, they were as peaceful and unwarlike in their habits as the Quakers themselves. They had been subjugated by the Five Nations, forced to take the appellation of squaws, and forgo the use of arms; but after they moved west, beyond the influence of their former masters, their naturally independent spirit revived, they soon regained their lofty position as braves and warriors, and the male squaws of the Iroquois soon became formidable men and heroes, and so have continued to the present day. Their warpath has reached the shores of the Pacific Ocean on the west, Hudson's Bay on the north, and into the very heart of Mexico on the south.

They are not clannish in their dispositions like most other Indians, nor by their habits confined to any given locality, but are found as traders, trappers, or hunters among most of the Indian tribes inhabiting our continent. I even saw them living with the Mormons in Utah. They are among the Indians as the Jews among the whites, essentially wanderers.

The Shawnees have been associated with the Delawares 185 years. They intermarry and live as one people. Their present places of abode are upon the Missouri River, near Fort Leavenworth, and in the Choctaw Territory, upon the Canadian River, near Fort Arbuckle. They are familiar with many of the habits and customs of their pale-faced neighbors, and some of them speak the English language, yet many of their native characteristics tenaciously cling to them.

Upon one occasion I endeavored to teach a Delaware the use of the compass. He seemed much interested in its mechanism, and very attentively observed the oscillations of the needle. He would move away a short distance, then return, keeping his eyes continually fixed upon the needle and the uniform position into which it settled. He did not, however, seem to comprehend it in the least, but regarded the entire proceeding as a species of necromantic performance got up for his especial benefit, and I was about putting away the instrument when he motioned me to stop, and came walking toward it with a very serious but incredulous countenance, remarking, as he pointed his finger toward it, "Maybe so he tell lie sometime."

The ignorance evinced by this Indian regarding the uses of the compass is less remarkable than that of some white men who are occasionally met upon the frontier.

While surveying Indian lands in the wilds of

Western Texas during the summer of 1854, I encountered a deputy surveyor traveling on foot, with his compass and chain upon his back. I saluted him very politely, remarking that I presumed he was a surveyor, to which he replied, "I reckon, *stranger,* I ar that thar individoal."

I had taken the magnetic variation several times, always with nearly the same results (about 10° 20'); but, in order to verify my observations, I was curious to learn how they accorded with his own working, and accordingly inquired of him what he made the variation of he compass in that particular locality. He seemed struck with astonishment, took his compass from his back and laid it upon a log nearby, then facing me, and pointing with his hand toward it, said,

"Straanger, do yer see that thar instru-*ment?*" to which I replied in the affirmative. He continued,

"I've owned her well-nigh goin on twenty year. I've put her through the perarries and through the timber, and now look yeer, straanger, you can just bet your life on't she never *var*-ried arry time, and if you'll just follow her sign you'll knock the center outer the north star. She never lies, she don't."

He seemed to consider my interrogatory as a direct insinuation that his compass was an imperfect one, and hence his indignation. Thinking that I should not get any very important intelligence concerning the variation of the needle from this surveyor, I begged his pardon for questioning the accuracy of his instru-*ment,* bid him good morning, and continued on my journey.

BLACK BEAVER.

In 1849 I met with a very interesting specimen of the Delaware tribe whose name was Black Beaver. He had for ten years been in the employ of the American Fur Company, and during this time had visited nearly every point of interest within the limits of our unsettled territory. He had set his traps and spread his blanket upon the headwaters of the Missouri and Columbia; and his wanderings had led him south to the Colorado and Gila, and thence to the shores of the Pacific in Southern California. His life had been that of a veritable cosmopolite, filled with scenes of intense and startling interest, bold and reckless adventure. He was with me two seasons in the capacity of guide, and I always found him perfectly reliable, brave, and competent. His reputation as a resolute, determined, and fearless warrior did not admit of question, yet I have never seen a man who wore his laurels with less vanity.

When I first made his acquaintance I was puzzled to know what to think of him. He would often, in speaking of the Prairie Indians, say to me,

"Captain, if you have a fight, you mustn't count much on me, for I'ze a big coward. When the fight begins I 'spect you'll see me run under the cannon; Injun mighty 'fraid of big gun."

I expressed my surprise that he should, if what he told me was true, have gained such a reputation as a warrior; whereupon he informed me that many years previous, when he was a young man, and before he had ever been in battle, he, with about twenty white men and four Delawares, were at one of the Fur Company's trading posts upon the Upper Missouri, engaged in trapping beaver. While there, the stockade fort was attacked by a numerous band of Blackfeet Indians, who fought bravely, and seemed determined to annihilate the little band that defended it.

After the investment had been completed, and there appeared no probability of the attacking party's abandoning their purpose, "One d——d fool Delaware" (as Black Beaver expressed it) proposed to his countrymen to make a sortie, and thereby endeavor to effect an impression upon the Blackfeet. This, Beaver said, was the last thing he would ever have thought of suggesting, and it startled him prodigiously, causing him to tremble so much that it was with difficulty he could stand.

He had, however, started from home with the fixed purpose of becoming a distinguished brave, and made a great effort to stifle his emotion. He assumed an air of determination, saying that was the very idea he was just about to propose; and, slapping his comrades upon the back, started toward the gate, telling them to follow. As soon as the gate was passed, he says, he took particular care to keep in the rear of the others, so that, in the event of a retreat, he would be able to reach the stockade first.

They had not proceeded far before a perfect shower of arrows came falling around them on all sides, but, fortunately, without doing them harm. Not fancying this hot reception, those in front proposed an immediate retreat, to which he most gladly acceded, and at once set off at his utmost speed, expecting to reach the fort first. But he soon discovered that his comrades were more fleet, and were rapidly passing and leaving him behind. Suddenly he stopped and called out to them, "Come back here, you cowards, you squaws; what for you run away and leave brave man to fight alone?" This taunting appeal to their courage turned them back, and, with their united efforts, they succeeded in beating off the enemy immediately around them, securing their entrance into the fort.

Beaver says when the gate was closed the captain in charge of the establishment grasped him warmly by the hand, saying, "Black Beaver, you are a brave man; you have done this day what no other man in the fort would have the courage to do, and I thank you from the bottom of my heart."

In relating the circumstance to me he laughed most heartily, thinking it a very good joke, and said after that he was regarded as a brave warrior.

The truth is, my friend Beaver was one of those few heroes who never sounded his own trumpet; yet no one that knows him ever presumed to question his courage.

At another time, while Black Beaver remained upon the headwaters of the Missouri, he was left in charge of a "cache" consisting of a quantity of goods buried to prevent their being stolen by the Indians. During the time he was engaged upon this duty he amused himself by hunting in the vicinity, only visiting his charge once a day. As he was making one of these periodical visits, and had arrived upon the summit of a hill overlooking the locality, he suddenly discovered a large number of hostile Blackfeet occupying it, and he supposed they had appropriated all the goods. As soon as they espied him, they beckoned for him to come down and have a friendly chat with them.

Knowing that their purpose was to beguile him into their power, he replied that he did not feel in a talking humor just at that time, and started off in another direction, whereupon they hallooed after him, making use of the most insulting language and gestures, and asking him if he considered himself a man thus to run away from his friends, and intimating that, in their opinion, he was an old woman, who had better go home and take care of the children.

Beaver says this roused his indignation to such a pitch that he stopped, turned around, and replied, "Maybe so; s'pose three or four of you Injuns come up here alone, I'll show you if I'ze old womans." They did not, however, accept the challenge, and Beaver rode off.

Although the Delawares generally seem quite

happy in their social relations, yet they are not altogether exempt from some of those minor discords which occasionally creep in and mar the domestic harmony of their more civilized pale-faced brethren.

I remember, upon one occasion, I had bivouacked for the night with Black Beaver, and he had been endeavoring to while away the long hours of the evening by relating to me some of the most thrilling incidents of his highly adventurous and erratic life, when at length a hiatus in the conversation gave me an opportunity of asking him if he was a married man. He hesitated for some time; then looking up and giving his forefinger a twirl, to imitate the throwing of a lasso, replied, "One time me catch 'um wife. I pay that woman, *his modder,* one hoss—one saddle—one bridle—two plug tobacco, and plenty goods. I take him home to my house—got plenty meat—plenty corn—plenty everything. One time me go to take walk, maybe so three, maybe so two hours. When I come home, that woman he say, 'Black Beaver, what for you go way long time?' I say, 'I not go nowhere; I just take one littel walk.' Then that woman he get heap mad, and say, 'No, Black Beaver, you not take no littel walk. I know what for you go way; *you go see nodder one woman.*' I say, 'Maybe not.' Then that woman she cry long time, and all e'time now she mad. You never seen 'Merican woman that a-way?"

I sympathized most deeply with my friend in his distress, and told him for his consolation that, in my opinion, the women of his nation were not peculiar in this respect; that they were pretty much alike all over the world, and I was under the impression that there were well-authenticated instances even among white women where they had subjected themselves to the same causes of complaint so feelingly depicted by him. Whereupon he very earnestly asked, "What you do for cure him? Whip him?" I replied, "No; that, so far as my observation extended, I was under the impression that this was generally regarded by those who had suffered from its effects as one of those chronic and vexatious complaints which would not be benefited by the treatment he suggested, even when administered in homeopathic doses, and I believed it was now admitted by all sensible men that it was better in all such cases to let nature take its course, trusting to a merciful Providence."

At this reply his countenance assumed a dejected expression, but at length he brightened up again and triumphantly remarked, "I tell you, my friend, what I do; I ketch 'um nodder one wife when I go home."

Black Beaver had visited St. Louis and the small towns upon the Missouri frontier, and he prided himself not a little upon his acquaintance with the customs of the whites, and never seemed more happy than when an opportunity offered to display this knowledge in presence of his Indian companions. It so happened, upon one occasion, that I had a Comanche guide who bivouacked at the same fire with Beaver. On visiting them one evening according to my usual practice, I found them engaged in a very earnest and apparently not very amicable conversation. On inquiring the cause of this, Beaver answered,

"I've been telling this Comanche what I seen 'mong the white folks."

"I said, "Well, Beaver, what did you tell him?"

"I tell him 'bout the steamboats, and the railroads, and the heap o' houses I seen in St. Louis."

"Well, sir, what does he think of that?"

"He say I'ze d——d fool."

"What else did you tell him about?"

"I tell him the world is round, but he keep all e'time say, Hush, you fool! do you spose I'ze child? Haven't I got eyes? Can't I see the prairie? You call him round? He say, too, maybe so I tell you something you not know before. One time my grandfather he make long journey that way (pointing to the west). When he get on big mountain, he seen heap water on t'other side, jest so flat he can be, and he seen the sun go right straight down on t'other side. I then tell him all these rivers he seen, all e'time the water he run; s'pose the world flat the water he stand still. Maybe so he not b'lieve me?"

I told him it certainly looked very much like it. I then asked him to explain to the Comanche the magnetic telegraph. He looked at me earnestly, and said,

"What you call that magnetic telegraph?"

I said, "You have heard of New York and New Orleans?"

"Oh yes," he replied.

"Very well; we have a wire connecting these two cities, which are about a thousand miles apart, and it would take a man thirty days to ride it upon a good horse. Now a man stands at one end of this wire in New York, and by touching it a few times he inquires of his friend in New Orleans what he had for breakfast. His friend in New Orleans touches the other end of the wire, and in ten minutes the answer comes back—ham and eggs. Tell him that, Beaver."

His countenance assumed a most comical expression, but he made no remark until I again requested him to repeat what I had said to the Comanche, when he observed,

"No, captain, I not tell him that, for I don't b'lieve that myself."

Upon my assuring him that such was the fact, and that I had seen it myself, he said,

"Injun not very smart; sometimes he's big fool, but he holler pretty loud; you hear him maybe half a mile; you say 'Merican man he talk thousand miles. I 'spect you try to fool me now, captain; *maybe so you lie.*"

The Indians living between the outer white settlements and the nomadic tribes of the Plains form intermediate social links in the chain of civilization.

The first of these occupy permanent habitations, but the others, although they cultivate the soil, are only resident while their crops are growing, going out into the prairies after harvest to spend the winter in hunting. Among the former may be mentioned the Cherokees, Creeks, Choctaws, and Chickasaws, and of the latter are the Delawares, Shawnees, Kickapoos, etc., who are perfectly familiar with the use of the rifle, and, in my judgment, would make as formidable partisan warriors as can be found in the universe.

THE WILD TRIBES OF THE WEST.

These are very different in their habits from the natives that formerly occupied the country bordering upon the Atlantic coast. The latter lived permanently in villages, where they cultivated the soil, and never wandered very far from them. They did not use horses, but always made their war expeditions on foot, and never came into action unless they could screen themselves behind the cover of trees. They inflicted the most inhuman tortures upon their prisoners, but did not, that I am aware, violate the chastity of women.

The prairie tribes have no permanent abiding places; they never plant a seed, but roam for hundreds of miles in every direction over the Plains. They are perfect horsemen, and seldom go to war on foot. Their attacks are made in the open prairies, and when unhorsed they are powerless. They do not, like the eastern Indians, inflict upon their prisoners prolonged tortures, but invariably subject all females that have the misfortune to fall into their merciless clutches to an ordeal worse than death.

It is highly important to every man passing through a country frequented by Indians to know some of their habits, customs, and propensities, as this will facilitate his intercourse with friendly tribes, and enable him, when he wishes to avoid a conflict, to take precautions against coming in collision with those who are hostile.

Almost every tribe has its own way of constructing its lodges, encamping, making fires, its own style of dress, by some of which peculiarities the experienced frontiersman can generally distinguish them.

The Osages, for example, make their lodges in the shape of a wagon top, of bent rods or willows covered with skins, blankets, or the bark of trees.

The Kickapoo lodges are made in an oval form, something like a rounded haystack, of poles set in the ground, bent over, and united at top; this is covered with cloths or bark.

The Witchetaws, Wacos, Towackanies, and Tonkowas erect their hunting lodges of sticks put up in the form of the frustum of a cone and covered with brush.

All these tribes leave the framework of their lodges standing when they move from camp to camp, and this, of course, indicates the particular tribe that erected them.

The Delawares and Shawnees plant two upright forked poles, place a stick across them, and stretch a canvas covering over it, in the same manner as with the *tente d'abri*.

The Sioux, Arapahoes, Cheyennes, Utes, Snakes, Blackfeet, and Kioways make use of the Comanche lodge, covered with dressed buffalo hides.

All the Prairie Indians I have met with are the most inveterate beggars. They will flock around strangers, and, in the most importunate manner, ask for everything they see, especially tobacco and sugar; and, if allowed, they will handle, examine, and occasionally pilfer such things as happen to take their fancy. The proper way to treat them is to give them at once such articles as are to be disposed of, and then, in a firm and decided manner, let them understand that they are to receive nothing else.

A party of Keechis once visited my camp with their principal chief, who said he had some important business to discuss, and demanded a council with the *capitan.* After consent had been given, he assembled his principal men, and, going through the usual preliminary of taking a *big smoke,* he arose, and with a great deal of ceremony commenced his pompous and flowery speech, which, like all others of a similar character, amounted to nothing, until he touched upon the real object of his visit. He said he had traveled a long distance over the prairies to see and have a talk with his white brothers; that his people were very hungry and naked. He then approached me with six small sticks, and, after shaking hands, laid one of the sticks in my hand, which he said represented sugar, another signified tobacco, and the other four, pork, flour, whisky, and blankets, all of which he assured me his people were in great need of, and must have. His talk was then concluded, and he sat down, apparently much gratified with the graceful and impressive manner with which he had executed his part of the performance.

It then devolved upon me to respond to the brilliant effort of the prairie orator, which I did in something like the following manner. After imitating his style for a short time, I closed my remarks by telling him that we were poor infantry soldiers, who were always obliged to go on foot; that we had become very tried of walking, and would like very much to ride. Furthermore, I had observed that they had among them many fine horses and mules. I then took two small sticks, and imitating as nearly as possible the manner of the chief, placed one in his hand, which I told him was nothing more or less than a first-rate horse, and then the other, which signified a good large mule. I closed by saying that I was ready to exchange presents whenever it suited his convenience.

They looked at each other for some time without speaking, but finally got up and walked away, and I was not troubled with them again.

INDIAN FIGHTING.

The military system, as taught and practiced in our army up to the time of the Mexican war, was, without doubt, efficient and well adapted to the art of war among civilized nations. This system was designed for the operations of armies acting in populated districts, furnishing ample resources, and against an enemy who was tangible, and made use of a similar system.

The vast expanse of desert territory that has been annexed to our domain within the last few years is peopled by numerous tribes of marauding and erratic savages, who are mounted upon fleet and hardy horses, making war the business and pastime of their lives, and acknowledging none of the ameliorating conventionalities of civilized warfare. Their tactics are such as to render the old system almost wholly impotent.

To act against an enemy who is here today and there tomorrow; who at one time stampedes a herd of mules upon the headwaters of the Arkansas, and when next heard from is in the very heart of the populated districts of Mexico, laying waste haciendas, and carrying devastation, rapine, and murder in his steps; who is everywhere without being anywhere; who assembles at the moment of combat, and vanishes whenever fortune turns against him; who leaves his women and children far distant from the theater of hostilities, and has neither towns or magazines to defend, nor lines of retreat to cover; who derives his commissariat from the country he operates in, and is not encumbered with baggage wagons or pack trains; who comes into action only when it suits his purposes, and never without the advantage of numbers or position—with such an enemy the strategic science of civilized nations loses much of its importance, and finds but rarely, and only in peculiar localities, an opportunity to be put in practice.

Our little army, scattered as it has been over the vast area of our possessions, in small garrisons of one or two companies each, has seldom been in a situation to act successfully on the offensive against large numbers of these marauders, and has often been condemned to hold itself almost exclusively upon the defensive. The morale of the troops must thereby necessarily be seriously impaired, and the confidence of the savages correspondingly augmented. The system of small garrisons has a tendency to disorganize the troops in proportion as they are scattered, and renders them correspondingly inefficient. The same results have been observed by the French army in Algeria, where, in 1845, their troops were, like ours, disseminated over a vast space, and broken up into small detachments stationed in numerous entrenched posts. Upon the sudden appearance of Abd el Kader in the plain of Mitidja, they were defeated with serious losses, and were from day to day obliged to abandon these useless stations, with all the supplies they contained. A French writer, in discussing this subject, says:

> We have now abandoned the fatal idea of defending Algeria by small entrenched posts. In studying the character of the war, the nature of the men who are to oppose us, and of the country in which we are to operate, we must be convinced of the danger of admitting any other system of fortification than that which is to receive our grand depots, our magazines, and to serve as places to recruit and rest our troops when exhausted by long expeditionary movements.
>
> These fortifications should be established in the midst of the centers of action, so as to command the principal routes, and serve as pivots to expeditionary columns.
>
> We owe our success to a system of war which has its proofs in twice changing our relations with the Arabs. This system consists altogether in the great mobility we have given to our troops. Instead of disseminating our soldiers with the vain hope of protecting our frontiers with a line of small posts, we have concentrated them, to have them at all times ready for emergencies, and since then the fortune of the Arabs has waned, and we have marched from victory to victory.
>
> This system, which has thus far succeeded, ought to succeed always, and to conduct us, God willing, to the peaceful possession of the country.

In reading a treatise upon war as it is practiced by the French in Algeria, by Colonel A. Laure, of the 2d Algerine Tirailleurs, published in Paris in

1858, I was struck with the remarkable similarity between the habits of the Arabs and those of the wandering tribes that inhabit our Western prairies. Their manner of making war is almost precisely the same, and a successful system of strategic operations for one will, in my opinion, apply to the other.

As the Turks have been more successful than the French in their military operations against the Arab tribes, it may not be altogether uninteresting to inquire by what means these inferior soldiers have accomplished the best results.

The author above mentioned, in speaking upon this subject, says:

> In these latter days the world is occupied with the organization of mounted infantry, according to the example of the Turks, where, in the most successful experiments that have been made, the mule carries the foot-soldier.
>
> The Turkish soldier mounts his mule, puts his provisions upon one side and his accoutrements upon the other, and, thus equipped, sets out upon long marches, traveling day and night, and only reposing occasionally in bivouac. Arrived near the place of operations (as near the break of day as possible), the Turks dismount in the most profound silence, and pass in succession the bridle of one mule through that of another in such a manner that a single man is sufficient to hold forty or fifty of them by retaining the last bridle, which secures all the others; they then examine their arms, and are ready to commence their work. The chief gives his last orders,

posts his guides, and they make the attack, surprise the enemy, generally asleep, and carry the position without resistance. The operation terminated, they hasten to beat a retreat, to prevent the neighboring tribes from assembling, and thus avoid a combat.

The Turks had only three thousand mounted men and ten thousand infantry in Algeria, yet these thirteen thousand men sufficed to conquer the same obstacles which have arrested us for twenty-six years, notwithstanding the advantage we had of an army which was successively reenforced until it amounted to a hundred thousand.

Why not imitate the Turks, then, mount our infantry upon mules, and reduce the strength of our army?

The response is very simple:

The Turks are Turks—that is to say, Mussulmans—and indigenous to the country; the Turks speak the Arabic language; the Deys of Algiers had less country to guard than we, and they care very little about retaining possession of it. They are satisfied to receive a part of its revenues. They were not permanent; their dominion was held by a thread. The Arab dwells in tents; his magazines are in caves. When he starts upon a war expedition, he folds his tent, drives far away his beasts of burden, which transport his effects, and only carries with him his horse and arms. Thus equipped, he goes everywhere; nothing arrests him; and often, when we believe him twenty leagues distant, he is in ambush at precisely rifle range from the flanks of his enemy.

It may be thought the union of contingents might retard their movements, but this is not so. The

> Arabs, whether they number ten or a hundred thousand, move with equal facility. They go where they wish and as they wish upon a campaign; the place of rendezvous merely is indicated, and they arrive there.
>
> What calculations can be made against such an organization as this?
>
> Strategy evidently loses its advantages against such enemies; a general can only make conjectures; he marches to find the Arabs, and finds them not; then, again, when he least expects it, he suddenly encounters them.
>
> When the Arab despairs of success in battle, he places his sole reliance upon the speed of his horse to escape destruction; and as he is always in a country where he can make his camp beside a little water, he travels until he has placed a safe distance between himself and his enemy.

No people probably on the face of the earth are more ambitious of martial fame, or entertain a higher appreciation for the deeds of a daring and successful warrior, than the North American savages. The attainment of such reputation is the paramount and absorbing object of their lives; all their aspirations for distinction invariably take this channel of expression. A young man is never considered worthy to occupy a seat in council until he has encountered an enemy in battle; and he who can count the greatest number of scalps is the most highly honored by his tribe. This idea is inculcated from their earliest infancy. It is not surprising, therefore, that, with such weighty inducements before him, the young man who, as yet, has gained no renown as a brave or warrior, should be less discriminate in his attacks than older men who have already acquired a name. The young braves should, therefore, be closely watched when encountered on the Plains.

The prairie tribes are seldom at peace with all their neighbors, and some of the young braves of a tribe are almost always absent upon a war excursion. These forays sometimes extend into the heart of the northern states of Mexico, where the Indians have carried on successful invasions for many years. They have devastated and depopulated a great portion of Sonora and Chihuahua. The objects of these forays are to steal horses and mules, and to take prisoners; and if it so happens that a war party has been unsuccessful in the accomplishment of these ends or has had the misfortune to lose some of its number in battle, they become reckless, and will often attack a small party with whom they are not at war, provided they hope to escape detection. The disgrace attendant upon a return to their friends without some trophies as an offset to the loss of their comrades is a powerful incentive to action, and they extend but little mercy to defenseless travelers who have the misfortune to encounter them at such a conjuncture.

While en route from New Mexico to Arkansas in 1849 I was encamped near the head of the Colorado

River, and wishing to know the character of the country for a few miles in advance of our position, I desired an officer to go out and make the reconnoissance. I was lying sick in my bed at the time, or I should have performed the duty myself. I expected the officer would have taken an escort with him, but he omitted to do so, and started off alone. After proceeding a short distance he discovered four mounted Indians coming at full speed directly toward him, when, instead of turning his own horse toward camp, and endeavoring to make his escape (he was well mounted), or of halting and assuming a defensive attitude, he deliberately rode up to them; after which the tracks indicated that they proceeded about three miles together, when the Indians most brutally killed and scalped my most unfortunate but too credulous friend, who might probably have saved his life had he not, in the kindness of his excellent heart, imagined that the savages would reciprocate his friendly advances. He was most woefully mistaken, and his life paid the forfeit of his generous and noble disposition.

I have never been able to get any positive information as to the persons who committed this murder, yet circumstances render it highly probable that they were a party of young Indians who were returning from an unsuccessful foray, and they were unable to resist the temptation of taking the scalp and horse of the lieutenant.

A small number of white men, in traveling upon

the Plains, should not allow a party of strange Indians to approach them unless able to resist an attack under the most unfavorable circumstances.

It is a safe rule, when a man finds himself alone in the prairies, and sees a party of Indians approaching, not to allow them to come near him, and if they persist in so doing, to signal them to keep away. If they do not obey, and he be mounted upon a fleet horse, he should make for the nearest timber. If the Indians follow and press him too closely, he should halt, turn around, and point his gun at the foremost, which will often have the effect of turning them back, but he should never draw trigger unless he finds that his life depends upon the shot; for, as soon as his shot is delivered, his sole dependence, unless he have time to reload, must be upon the speed of his horse.

The Indians of the Plains, notwithstanding the encomiums that have been heaped upon their brethren who formerly occupied the Eastern States for their gratitude, have not, so far as I have observed, the most distant conception of that sentiment. You may confer numberless benefits upon them for years, and the more that is done for them the more they will expect. They do not seem to comprehend the motive which dictates an act of benevolence or charity, and they invariably attribute it to fear or the expectation of reward. When they make a present, it is with a view of getting more than its equivalent in return.

KEEP AWAY!

I have never yet been able to discover that the Western wild tribes possessed any of those attributes which among civilized nations are regarded as virtues adorning the human character. They have yet to be taught the first rudiments of civilization, and they are at this time as far from any knowledge of Christianity, and as worthy subjects for missionary enterprise, as the most untutored natives of the South Sea Islands.

The only way to make these merciless freebooters fear or respect the authority of our government is, when they misbehave, first of all to chastise them well by striking such a blow as will be felt for a long time, and thus show them that we are superior to them in war. They will then respect us much more than when their goodwill is purchased with presents.

The opinion of a friend of mine, who has passed the last twenty-five years of his life among the Indians of the Rocky Mountains, corroborates the opinions I have advanced upon this head, and although I do not endorse all of his sentiments, yet many of them are deduced from long and matured experience and critical observations. He says:

"They are the most onsartainest varmints in all creation, and I reckon tha'r not mor'n half human; for you never seed a human, arter you'd fed and treated him to the best fixins in your lodge, jist turn round and steal all your horses, or ary other thing he could lay his hands on. No, not adzackly. He would feel kinder grateful, and ask you to spread a blanket in his lodge ef you ever passed that a-way. But the Injun he don't care shucks for you, and is ready to do you a heap of mischief as soon as he quits your feed. No, Cap.," he continued, "it's not the right way to give um presents to buy peace; but ef I war governor of these yeer United States, I'll tell you what I'd do. I'd invite um all to a big feast, and make b'lieve I wanted to have a big talk; and as soon as I got um all together, I'd pitch in and sculp about half of um, and then t'other half would be mighty glad to make a peace that would stick. That's the way I'd make a treaty with the dog'ond, red-bellied varmints; and as sure as you're born, Cap., that's the only way."

I suggested to him the idea that there would be a lack of good faith and honor in such a proceeding, and that it would be much more in accordance with my notions of fair dealing to meet them openly in the field, and there endeavor to punish them if they deserve it. To this, he replied,

"Tain't no use to talk about honor with them, Cap.; they hain't got no such thing in um; and they won't show fair fight, any way you can fix it. Don't they kill and sculp a white man when-ar they get the better on him? The mean varmints, they'll never behave themselves until you give um a clean out-and-out licking. They can't onderstand white folks' ways, and they won't learn um; and ef you treat um decently, they think you ar afeard. You may depend on't, Cap., the only way to treat Injuns is to thrash them well at first, then the balance will sorter take to you and behave themselves."

The wealth of the Prairie Indians consists almost exclusively in their horses, of which they possess large numbers; and they are in the saddle from infancy to old age. Horsemanship is with them, as with the Arab of the Sahara, a necessary part of their education. The country they occupy is unsuited to cultivation, and their only avocations are war, rapine, and the chase. They have no fixed habitations, but move from place to place with the seasons and the game. All their worldly effects are transported in their migrations, and wherever their lodges are pitched there is their home. They are strangers to all cares, creating for themselves no artificial wants, and are perfectly happy and contented so long as the buffalo is found within the limits of their wanderings. Every man is a soldier, and they generally exhibit great confidence in their own military prowess.

MEETING INDIANS.

On approaching strangers these people put their horses at full speed, and persons not familiar with their peculiarities and habits might interpret this as an act of hostility; but it is their custom with friends as well as enemies, and should not occasion groundless alarm.

When a party is discovered approaching thus, and are near enough to distinguish signals, all that is necessary in order to ascertain their disposition is to raise the right hand with the palm in front, and gradually push it forward and back several times. They all understand this to be a command to halt, and if they are not hostile it will at once be obeyed.

After they have stopped the right hand is raised again as before, and slowly moved to the right and left, which signifies "I do now know you. Who are you?" As all the wild tribes have their peculiar pantomimic signals by which they are known, they will then answer the inquiry by giving their signal. If this should not be understood, they may be asked if they are friends by raising both hands grasped in the manner of shaking hands, or by locking the two forefingers firmly while the hands are held up. If friendly, they will respond with the same signal; but if enemies, they will probably disregard the command to halt, or give the signal of anger by closing the hand, placing it against the forehead, and turning it back and forth while in that position.

The pantomimic vocabulary is understood by all the Prairie Indians, and when oral communication is impracticable it constitutes the court or general council language of the Plains. The signs are exceedingly graceful and significant; and, what was a fact of much astonishment to me, I discovered they were very nearly the same as those practiced by the mutes in our deaf and dumb schools, and were comprehended by them with perfect facility.

The Comanche is represented by making with the hand a waving motion in imitation of the crawling of a snake.

The Cheyenne, or "Cut-arm," by drawing the hand across the arm, to imitate cutting it with a knife.

The Arapahoes, or "Smellers," by seizing the nose with the thumb and forefinger.

The Sioux, or "Cut-throats," by drawing the hand across the throat.

The Pawnees, or "Wolves," by placing a hand on each side of the forehead, with two fingers pointing to the front, to represent the narrow, sharp ears of the wolf.

The Crows, by imitating the flapping of the bird's wings with the palms of the hands.

When Indians meet a party of strangers, and are disposed to be friendly, the chiefs, after the usual salutations have been exchanged, generally ride out and accompany the commander of the party some distance, holding a friendly talk, and, at the same time, indulging their curiosity by learning the news, etc. Phlegmatic and indifferent as they appear to be, they are very inquisitive and observing, and, at the same time, exceedingly circumspect and cautious about disclosing their own purposes.

They are always desirous of procuring, from whomsoever they meet, testimonials of their good behavior, which they preserve with great care, and exhibit upon all occasions to strangers as a guarantee of future good conduct.

On meeting with a chief of the Southern Comanches in 1849, after going through the usual ceremony of embracing, and assuring me that he was the best friend the Americans ever had among the Indians, he exhibited numerous certificates from the different white men he had met with, testifying to his friendly disposition. Among these was one that he desired me to read with special attention, as he said he was of the opinion that perhaps it might not be so complimentary in its character as some of the others. It was in these words:

"The bearer of this says he is a Comanche chief, named Senaco; that he is the biggest Indian and best friend the whites ever had; in fact, that he is a first-rate fellow; but I believe he is a d——d rascal, *so look out for him.*"

I smiled on reading the paper, and, looking up, found the chief's eyes intently fixed upon mine with an expression of the most earnest inquiry. I told him the paper was not as good as it might be, whereupon he destroyed it.

Five years after this interview I met Senaco again near the same place. He recognized me at once, and, much to my surprise, pronounced my name quite distinctly.

A circumstance which happened in my interview with the Indian shows their character for diplomatic policy.

I was about locating and surveying a reservation of land upon which the government designed to establish the Comanches, and was desirous of ascertaining whether they were disposed voluntarily to come into the measure. In this connection, I stated to him that their Great Father, the President, being anxious to improve their condition, was willing to give them a permanent location, where they could cultivate the soil, and, if they wished it, he would send white men to teach them the rudiments of agriculture, supply them with farming utensils, and all other requisites for living comfortably in their new homes. I then desired him to consult with his people, and let me know what their views were upon the subject.

After talking a considerable time with his head men, he rose to reply, and said, "He was very happy to learn that the President remembered his poor red children in the Plains, and he was glad to see me again, and hear from me that their Great Father was their friend; that he was also very much gratified to meet his agent who was present, and that he should remember with much satisfaction the agreeable interview we had had upon that occasion." After delivering himself of numerous other non-committal expressions of similar import, he closed his speech and took his seat without making the slightest allusion to the subject in question.

On reminding him of this omission, and again demanding from him a distinct and categorical answer, he, after a brief consultation with his people, replied that his talk was made and concluded, and he did not comprehend why it was that I wanted to open the subject anew. But, as I continued to press him for an answer, he at length said, "You come into our country and select a small patch of ground, around which you run a line, and tell us the President will make us a present of this to live upon, when everybody knows that the whole of this entire country, from the Red River to the Colorado, is now, and always has been, ours from time immemorial. I suppose, however, if the President tells us to confine ourselves to these narrow limits, we shall be forced to do so, whether we desire it or not."

He was evidently averse to the proposed change in their mode of life, and has been at war ever since the establishment of the settlement.

The mode of life of the nomadic tribes, owing to their unsettled and warlike habits, is such as to render their condition one of constant danger and apprehension. The security of their numerous animals from the encroachments of their enemies and habitual liability to attacks compels them to be at all times upon the alert. Even during profound peace they guard their herds both night and day, while scouts are often patrolling upon the surrounding heights to give notice of the approach of strangers, and enable them to secure their animals and take a defensive attitude.

When one of these people conceives himself injured his thirst for revenge is insatiable. Grave and dignified in his outward bearing, and priding himself upon never exhibiting curiosity, joy, or anger, yet when once aroused he evinces the implacable dispositions of his race; the affront is laid up and cherished in his breast, and nothing can efface it from his mind until ample reparation is made. The insult must be atoned for by presents, or be washed out with blood.

WAR EXPEDITIONS.

When a chief desires to organize a war party, he provides himself with a long pole, attaches a red flag to the end of it, and trims the top with eagle feathers. He then mounts his horse in his war costume, and rides around through the camp singing the war song. Those who are disposed to join the expedition mount their horses and fall into the procession; after parading about for a time, all dismount, and the war dance is performed. This ceremony is continued from day to day until a sufficient number of volunteers are found to accomplish the objects desired, when they set out for the theater of their intended exploits.

As they proceed upon their expedition, it sometimes happens that the chief with whom it originated, and who invariably assumes the command, becomes discouraged at not finding an opportunity of displaying his warlike abilities, and abandons the enterprise; in which event, if others of the party desire to proceed farther, they select another leader and push on, and thus so long as any one of the party holds out.

A war party is sometimes absent for a great length of time, and for days, weeks, and months their friends at home anxiously await their return, until, suddenly, from afar, the shrill war cry of an *avant courier* is heard proclaiming the approach of the victorious warriors. The camp is in an instant alive with excitement and commotion. Men, women, and children swarm out to meet the advancing party. Their white horses are painted and decked out in the most fantastic style, and led in advance of the triumphal procession; and, as they pass around through the village, the old women set up a most unearthly howl of exultation, after which the scalp dance is performed with all the pomp and display their limited resources admit of, the warriors having their faces painted black.

When, on the other hand, the expedition terminates disastrously by the loss of some of the party in battle, the relatives of the deceased cut off their own hair, and the tails and manes of their horses, as symbols of mourning, and howl and cry for a long time.

In 1854 I saw the widow of a former chief of the Southern Comanches, whose husband had been dead about three years, yet she continued her mourning tribute to his memory by crying daily for him and refusing all offers to marry again.

The prairie warrior is occasionally seen with the rifle in his hand, but his favorite arm is the bow, the use of which is taught him at an early age. By constant practice he acquires a skill in archery that renders him no less formidable in war than successful in the chase. Their bows are usually made of the tough and elastic wood of the *bois d'are,* strengthened and reenforced with sinews of the deer wrapped firmly around, and strung with a cord of the same material. They are from three to four feet long. The arrows, which are carried in a quiver upon the back, are about twenty inches long, of flexible wood, with a triangular iron point at one end, and at the other two feathers intersecting at right angles.

At short distances (about fifty yards), the bow, in the hands of the Indian, is effective, and in close proximity with the buffalo throws the arrow entirely through his huge carcass. In using this weapon the warrior protects himself from the missiles of his enemy with a shield made of two thicknesses of undressed buffalo hide filled in with hair.

The Comanches, Sioux, and other prairie tribes make their attacks upon the open prairies. Trusting to their wonderful skill in equitation and horsemanship, they ride around their enemies with their bodies thrown upon the opposite side of the horse, and discharge their arrows in rapid succession while at full speed; they will not, however, often venture near an enemy who occupies a defensive position. If, therefore, a small party be in danger of an attack from a large force of Indians, they should seek the cover of timber or a park of wagons, or, in the absence of these, rocks or holes in the prairie which afford good cover.

Attempts to stampede animals are often made when parties first arrive in camp, and when everyone's attention is preoccupied in the arrangements therewith connected. In a country infested by hostile Indians, the ground in the vicinity of which it is proposed to encamp should be cautiously examined for tracks and other Indian signs by making a circuit around the locality previous to unharnessing the animals.

After Indians have succeeded in stampeding a herd of horses or mules, and desire to drive them away, they are in the habit of pushing them forward as rapidly as possible for the first few days, in order to place a wide interval between themselves and any party that may be in pursuit.

In running off stolen animals, the Indians are generally divided into two parties, one for driving and the other to act as a rear guard. Before they reach a place where they propose making a halt, they leave a vidette upon some prominent point to watch for pursuers and give the main party timely warning, enabling them to rally their animals and push forward again.

TRACKING INDIANS.

When an Indian sentinel intends to watch for an enemy approaching from the rear, he selects the highest position available, and places himself near the summit in such an attitude that his entire body shall be concealed from the observation of anyone in the rear, his head only being exposed above the top of the eminence. Here he awaits with great patience so long as he thinks there is any possibility of danger, and it will be difficult for an enemy to surprise him or to elude his keen and scrutinizing vigilance. Meanwhile his horse is secured under the screen of the hill, all ready when required. Hence it will be evident that, in following Indian depredators, the utmost vigilance and caution must be exercised to conceal from them the movements of their pursuers. They are the best scouts in the world, proficient in all the artifices and stratagems available in border warfare, and when hotly pursued by a superior force, after exhausting all other means of evasion, they scatter in different directions; and if, in a broken or mountainous country, they can do no better, abandon their horses and baggage, and take refuge in the rocks, gorges, or other hiding places. This plan has several times been resorted to by Indians in Texas when surprised, and, notwithstanding their pursuers were directly upon them, the majority made their escape, leaving behind all their animals and other property.

For overtaking a marauding party of Indians who have advanced eight or ten hours before the pursuing party are in readiness to take the trail, it is not best to push forward rapidly at first, as this will weary and break down horses. The Indians must be supposed to have at least fifty or sixty miles the start; it will, therefore, be useless to think of overtaking them without providing for a long chase. Scouts should continually be kept out in front upon the trail to reconnoiter and give preconcerted signals to the main party when the Indians are espied.

In approaching all eminences or undulations in the prairies, the commander should be careful not to allow any considerable number of his men to pass upon the summits until the country around has been carefully reconnoitered by the scouts, who will cautiously raise their eyes above the crests of the most elevated points, making a scrutinizing examination in all directions; and, while doing this, should an Indian be encountered who has been left behind as a sentinel, he must, if possible, be secured or shot, to prevent his giving the alarm to his comrades. These precautions cannot be too rigidly enforced when the trail becomes "warm"; and if there be a moon, it will be better to lie by in the daytime and follow the trail at night, as the great object is to come upon the Indians when they are not anticipating an attack. Such surprises, if discreetly conducted, generally prove successful.

As soon as the Indians are discovered in their

bivouac, the pursuing party should dismount, leave their horses under charge of a guard in some sequestered place, and, before advancing to the attack, the men should be instructed in signals for their different movements, such as all will easily comprehend and remember. As, for example, a pull upon the right arm may signify to face to the right, and a pull upon the left arm to face to the left; a pull upon the skirt of the coat, to halt; a gentle push on the back, to advance in ordinary time; a slap on the back, to advance in double quick time, etc., etc.

These signals, having been previously well understood and practiced, may be given by the commander to the man next to him, and from him communicated in rapid succession throughout the command.

I will suppose the party formed in one rank, with the commander on the right. He gives the signal, and the men move off cautiously in the direction indicated. The importance of not losing sight of his comrades on his right and left, and of not allowing them to get out of his reach, so as to break the chain of communication, will be apparent to all, and great care should be taken that the men do not mistake their brothers in arms for the enemy. This may be prevented by having two passwords, and when there be any doubt as to the identity of two men who meet during the night operations, one of these words may be repeated by each. Above all, the men must be fully impressed with the importance of not firing a shot until the order is given by the commanding officer, and also that a rigorous personal accountability will be enforced in all cases of a violation of this rule.

If the commander gives the signal for commencing the attack by firing a pistol or gun, there will probably be no mistake, unless it happens through carelessness by the accidental discharge of firearms.

I can conceive of nothing more appalling, or that tends more to throw men off their guard and produce confusion, than a sudden and unexpected night attack. Even the Indians, who pride themselves upon their coolness and self-possession, are far from being exempt from its effects; and it is not surprising that men who go to sleep with a sense of perfect security around them, and are suddenly aroused from a sound slumber by the terrific sounds of an onslaught from an enemy, should lose their presence of mind.

TELEGRAPHING BY SMOKES.

The transparency of the atmosphere upon the Plains is such that objects can be seen at great distances; a mountain, for example, presents a distinct and bold outline at fifty or sixty miles, and may occasionally be seen as far as a hundred miles.

The Indians, availing themselves of this fact, have been in the habit of practicing a system of telegraphing by means of smokes during the day and fires by night, and, I daresay, there are but few travelers who have crossed the mountains to California that have not seen these signals made and responded to from peak to peak in rapid succession.

The Indians thus make known to their friends many items of information highly important to them. If enemies or strangers make their appearance in the country, the fact is telegraphed at once, giving them time to secure their animals and to prepare for attack, defense, or flight.

War or hunting parties, after having been absent a long time from their erratic friends at home, and not knowing where to find them, make use of the same preconcerted signals to indicate their presence.

Very dense smokes may be raised by kindling a large fire with dry wood, and piling upon it the green boughs of pine, balsam, or hemlock. This throws off a heavy cloud of black smoke which can be seen very far.

This simple method of telegraphing, so useful to the savages both in war and in peace, may, in my judgment, be used to advantage in the movements of troops cooperating in separate columns in the Indian country.

I shall not attempt at this time to present a matured system of signals, but will merely give a few suggestions tending to illustrate the advantages to be derived from the use of them.

For example, when two columns are marching through a country at such distances apart that smokes may be seen from one to the other, their respective positions may be made known to each other at any time by two smokes raised simultaneously or at certain preconcerted intervals.

Should the commander of one column desire to communicate with the other, he raises three smokes simultaneously, which, if seen by the other party, should be responded to in the same manner. They would then hold themselves in readiness for any other communications.

If an enemy is discovered in small numbers, a smoke raised twice at fifteen minutes' interval would indicate it; and if in large force, three times with the same intervals might be the signal.

Should the commander of one party desire the other to join him, this might be telegraphed by four smokes at ten minutes' interval.

Should it become necessary to change the direction of the line of march, the commander may transmit the order by means of two simultaneous smokes raised a certain number of times to indicate the particular direction; for instance, twice for north, three times for south, four times for east, and five times for west; three smokes raised twice for northeast, three times for northwest, etc., etc.

By multiplying the combinations of signals a great variety of messages might be transmitted in this manner; but, to avoid mistakes, the signals should be written down and copies furnished the commander of each separate party, and they need not necessarily be made known to other persons.

During the day an intelligent man should be detailed to keep a vigilant lookout in all directions for smokes, and he should be furnished with a watch, pencil, and paper, to make a record of the signals, with their number, and the time of the intervals between them.

CHAPTER VII.

Hunting.—Its Benefits to the Soldier.—Buffalo.—Deer.—Antelope.—Bear.—Bighorn, or Mountain Sheep.—Their Habits, and Hints upon the best Methods of hunting them.

HUNTING.

I KNOW of no better school of practice for perfecting men in target firing, and the use of firearms generally, than that in which the frontier hunter receives his education. One of the first and most important lessons that he is taught impresses him with the conviction that, unless his gun is in good order and steadily directed upon the game, he must go without his supper; and if ambition does not stimulate his efforts, his appetite will, and ultimately lead to success and confidence in his own powers.

The man who is afraid to place the butt of his piece firmly against his shoulder, or who turns away his head at the instant of pulling trigger (as soldiers often do before they have been drilled at target practice), will not be likely to bag much game or to contribute materially toward the result of a battle. The successful hunter, as a general rule, is a good shot, will always charge his gun properly, and may be relied upon in action. I would, therefore, when in garrison or at permanent camps, encourage officers and soldiers in field sports. If permitted, men very readily cultivate a fondness for these innocent and healthy exercises, and occupy their leisure time in their pursuit; whereas, if confined to the narrow limits of a frontier camp or garrison, having no amusements within their reach, they are prone to indulge in practices which are highly detrimental to their physical and moral condition.

By making short excursions about the country they acquire a knowledge of it, become inured to fatigue, learn the art of bivouacking, trailing, etc., etc., all of which will be found serviceable in border warfare; and, even if they should perchance now and then miss some of the minor routine duties of the garrison, the benefits they would derive from hunting would, in my opinion, more than counterbalance its effects. Under the old regime it was thought that drills, dress parades, and guard mountings comprehended the sum total of the soldier's education, but the experience of the last ten years has taught us that these are only the rudiments, and that to combat successfully with Indians we must receive instruction from them, study their tactics, and, where they suit our purposes, copy from them.

The union of discipline with the individuality, self-reliance, and rapidity of locomotion of the savage is what we should aim at. This will be the tendency of the course indicated, and it is conceived by the writer that an army composed of well-disciplined hunters will be the most efficient of all others against the only enemy we have to encounter within the limits of our vast possessions.

I find some pertinent remarks upon this subject in a very sensible essay by "a late captain of infantry" (U.S.). He says:

"It is conceived that scattered bands of mounted hunters, with the speed of a horse and the watchfulness of a wolf or antelope, whose faculties are sharpened by their necessities; who, when they get short of provisions, separate and look for something to eat, and find it in the water, in the ground, or on the surface; whose bill of fare ranges from grass seed, nuts, roots, grasshoppers, lizards, and rattlesnakes up to the antelope, deer, elk, bear, and buffalo, and who have a continent to roam over, will be neither surprised, caught, conquered, overawed, or reduced to famine by a rumbling, bugle-blowing, drum-beating town passing through their country on wheels at the speed of a loaded wagon.

"If the Indians are in the path and do not wish to be seen, they cross a ridge, and the town moves on, ignorant whether there are fifty Indians within a mile or no Indian within fifty miles. If the Indians wish to see, they return to the crest of the ridge, crawl up to the edge, pull up a bunch of grass by the roots, and look through or under it at the procession."

Although I would always encourage men in hunting when permanently located, yet, unless they are good woodsmen, it is not safe to permit them to go out alone in marching through the Indian country, as, aside from the danger of encountering Indians, they would be liable to become bewildered and perhaps lost, and this might detain the entire party in searching for them. The better plan upon a march is for three or four to go out together, accompanied by a good woodsman, who will be able with certainty to lead them back to camp.

The little group could ascertain if Indians are about, and would be strong enough to act on the defensive against small parties of them; and, while they are amusing themselves, they may perform an important part as scouts and flankers.

An expedition may have been perfectly organized, and everything provided that the wisest forethought could suggest, yet circumstances beyond the control of the most experienced traveler may sometimes arise to defeat the best concerted plans. It is not, for example, an impossible contingency that the traveler may, by unforeseen delays, consume his provisions, lose them in crossing streams, or have them stolen by hostile Indians, and be reduced to the necessity of depending upon game for subsistence. Under these circumstances, a few observations upon the habits of the different animals that frequent the Plains and on the best methods of hunting them may not be altogether devoid of interest or utility in this connection.

THE BUFFALO.

The largest and most useful animal that roams over the prairies is the buffalo. It provides food, clothing, and shelter to thousands of natives whose means of livelihood depend almost exclusively upon this gigantic monarch of the prairies.

Not many years since they thronged in countless multitudes over all that vast area lying between Mexico and the British possessions, but now their range is confined within very narrow limits, and a few more years will probably witness the extinction of the species.

The traveler, in passing from Texas or Arkansas through southern New Mexico to California, does not, at the present day, encounter the buffalo; but upon all the routes north of latitude 36° the animal is still found between the 99th and 102d meridians of longitude.

Although generally regarded as migratory in their habits, yet the buffalo often winter in the snows of a high northern latitude. Early in the spring of 1858 I found them in the Rocky Mountains, at the head of the Arkansas and South Platte rivers, and there was every indication that this was a permanent abiding place for them.

There are two methods generally practiced in hunting the buffalo, viz.: running them on horseback, and stalking, or still-hunting. The first method requires a surefooted and tolerably fleet horse that is not easily frightened. The buffalo cow, which makes much better beef than the bull, when pursued by the hunter runs rapidly, and, unless the horse be fleet, it requires a long and exhausting chase to overtake her.

When the buffalo are discovered, and the hunter intends to give chase, he should first dismount, arrange his saddle blanket and saddle, buckle the girth tight, and make every thing about his horse furniture snug and secure. He should then put his arms in good firing order, and, taking the lee side of the herd, so that they may not get "the wind" of him, he should approach in a walk as close as possible, taking advantage of any cover that may offer. His horse then, being cool and fresh, will be able to dash into the herd, and probably carry his rider very near the animal he has selected before he becomes alarmed.

If the hunter be right-handed, and uses a pistol, he should approach upon the left side, and when nearly opposite and close upon the buffalo, deliver his shot, taking aim a little below the center of the body, and about eight inches back of the shoulder. This will strike the vitals, and generally render another shot unnecessary.

When a rifle or shotgun is used the hunter rides up on the right side, keeping his horse well in hand, so as to be able to turn off if the beast charges upon him; this, however, never happens except with a buffalo that is wounded, when it is advisable to keep out of his reach.

The buffalo has immense powers of endurance, and will run for many miles without any apparent effort or diminution in speed. The first buffalo I ever saw I followed about ten miles, and when I left him he seemed to run faster than when the chase commenced.

As a long buffalo chase is very severe labor upon a horse, I would recommend to all travelers, unless they have a good deal of surplus horseflesh, never to expend it in running buffalo.

Still-hunting, which requires no consumption of horseflesh, and is equally successful with the other method, is recommended. In stalking on horseback, the most broken and hilly localities should be selected, as these will furnish cover to the hunter, who passes from the crest of one hill to another, examining the country carefully in all directions. When the game is discovered, if it happen to be on the lee side, the hunter should endeavor, by making a wide detour, to get upon the opposite side, as he will find it impossible to approach within rifle range with the wind.

When the animal is upon a hill, or in any other position where he cannot be approached without danger of disturbing him, the hunter should wait until he moves off to more favorable ground, and this will not generally require much time, as they wander about a great deal when not grazing; he then pickets his horse, and approaches cautiously, seeking to screen himself as much as possible by the undulations in the surface, or behind such other objects as may present themselves; but if the surface should offer no cover, he must crawl upon his hands and knees when near the game, and in this way he can generally get within rifle range.

Should there be several animals together, and his first shot take effect, the hunter can often get several other shots before they become frightened. A Delaware Indian and myself once killed five buffaloes out of a small herd before the remainder were so much disturbed as to move away, although we were within the short distance of twenty yards, yet the reports of our rifles did not frighten them in the least, and they continued grazing during all the time we were loading and firing.

The sense of smelling is exceedingly acute with the buffalo, and they will take the wind from the hunter at as great a distance as a mile.

When the animal is wounded, and stops, it is better not to go near him until he lies down, as he will often run a great distance if disturbed; but if left to himself, will in many cases die in a short time.

The tongues, humps, and marrow bones are regarded as the choice parts of the animal. The tongue is taken out by ripping open the skin between the prongs of the lower jawbone and pulling it out through the orifice. The hump may be taken off by skinning down on each side of the shoulders and cutting away the meat, after which the hump ribs can be unjointed where they unite with the spine. The marrow, when roasted in the bones, is delicious.

THE DEER.

Of all game quadrupeds indigenous to this continent, the common red deer is probably more widely dispersed from north to south and from east to west over our vast possessions than any other. They are found in all latitudes from Hudson's Bay to Mexico, and they clamber over the most elevated peaks of the western sierras with the same ease that they range the eastern forests or the everglades of Florida. In summer they crop the grass upon the summits of the Rocky Mountains, and in winter, when the snow falls deep, they descend into sheltered valleys, where they fall an easy prey to the Indians.

Besides the common red deer of the Eastern States, two other varieties are found in the Rocky Mountains, viz., the "black-tailed deer," which takes its name from the fact of its having a small tuft of black hair upon the end of its tail, and the "long-tailed" species. The former of these is considerably larger than the eastern deer, and is much darker, being of a very deep-yellowish iron-gray, with a yellowish red upon the belly. It frequents the mountains, and is never seen far away from them. Its habits are similar to those of the red deer, and it is hunted in the same way. The only difference I have been able to discern between the long-tailed variety and the common deer is in the length of the tail and body. I have seen this animal only in the neighborhood of the Rocky Mountains, but it may resort to other localities.

Although the deer are still abundant in many of our forest districts in the east, and do not appear to decrease very rapidly, yet there has within a few years been a very evident diminution in the numbers of those frequenting our Western prairies. In passing through Southern Texas in 1846, thousands of deer were met with daily, and, astonishing as it may appear, it was no uncommon spectacle to see from one to two hundred in a single herd; the prairies seemed literally alive with them; but in 1855 it was seldom that a herd of ten was seen in the same localities. It seemed to me that the vast herds first met with could not have been killed off by the hunters in that sparsely populated section, and I was puzzled to know what had become of them. It is possible they may have moved off into Mexico; they certainly are not in our territory at the present time.

Twenty years' experience in deer hunting has taught me several facts relative to the habits of the animal which, when well understood, will be found of much service to the inexperienced hunter, and greatly contribute to his success. The best target-shots are not necessarily the most skillful deer-stalkers. One of the great secrets of this art is in knowing how to approach the game without giving alarm, and this cannot easily be done unless the hunter sees it before he is himself discovered. There are so many objects in the woods resembling the deer in color that none but a practiced eye can often detect the difference.

When the deer is reposing he generally turns his head from the wind, in which position he can see an enemy approaching from that direction, and his nose will apprise him of the presence of danger from the opposite side. The best method of hunting deer, therefore, is *across the wind.*

While the deer are feeding, early in the morning and a short time before dark in the evening are the best times to stalk them, as they are then busily occupied and less on the alert. When a deer is espied with his head down, cropping the grass, the hunter advances cautiously, keeping his eyes constantly directed upon him, and screening himself behind intervening objects, or, in the absence of other cover, crawls along upon his hands and knees in the grass, until the deer hears his steps and raises his head, when he must instantly stop and remain in an attitude fixed and motionless as a statue, for the animal's vision is his keenest sense. When alarmed he will detect the slightest movement of a small object, and, unless the hunter stands or lies perfectly still, his presence will be detected. If the hunter does not move, the deer will, after a short time, recover from his alarm and resume his grazing, when he may be again approached. The deer always exhibits his alarm by a sudden jerking of the tail just before he raises his head.

I once saw a Delaware Indian walk directly up within rifle range of a deer that was feeding upon the open prairie and shoot him down; he was, however, a long time in approaching, and made frequent halts whenever the animal flirted his tail and raised his head. Although he often turned toward the hunter, yet he did not appear to notice him, probably taking him for a stump or tree.

When the deer are lying down in the smooth prairie, unless the grass is tall, it is difficult to get near them, as they are generally looking around, and become alarmed at the least noise.

The Indians are in the habit of using a small instrument which imitates the bleat of the young fawn, with which they lure the doe within range of their rifles. The young fawn gives out no scent upon its track until it is sufficiently grown to make good running, and instinct teaches the mother that this wise provision of nature to preserve the helpless little quadruped from the ravages of wolves, panthers, and other carnivorous beasts, will be defeated if she remains with it, as her tracks cannot be concealed. She therefore hides her fawn in the grass, where it is almost impossible to see it, even when very near it, goes off to some neighboring thicket within call, and makes her bed alone. The Indian pot-hunter, who is but little scrupulous as to the means he employs in accomplishing his ends, sounds the bleat along near the places where he thinks the game is lying, and the unsuspicious doe, who imagines that her offspring is in distress, rushes with headlong impetuosity toward the sound, and often goes within a few yards of the hunter to receive her death wound.

This is cruel sport, and can only be justified when meat is scarce, which is very frequently the case in the Indian's larder.

It does not always comport with a man's feelings of security, especially if he happens to be a little nervous, to sound the deer bleat in a wild region of country. I once undertook to experiment with the instrument myself, and made my first essay in attempting to call up an antelope which I discovered in the distance. I succeeded admirably in luring the wary victim within shooting range, had raised upon my knees, and was just in the act of pulling trigger, when a rustling in the grass on my left drew my attention in that direction, where, much to my surprise, I beheld a huge panther within about twenty yards, bounding with gigantic strides directly toward me. I turned my rifle, and in an instant, much to my relief and gratification, its contents were lodged in the heart of the beast.

Many men, when they suddenly encounter a deer, are seized with nervous excitement, called in sporting parlance the "buck fever," which causes them to fire at random. Notwithstanding I have had much experience in hunting, I must confess that I am never entirely free from some of the symptoms of this malady when firing at large game, and I believe that in four out of five cases where I have missed the game my balls have passed too high. I have endeavored to obviate this by sighting my rifle low, and it has been attended with more successful results. The same remarks apply to most other men I have met with. They fire too high when excited.

THE ANTELOPE.

This animal frequents the most elevated bleak and naked prairies in all latitudes from Mexico to Oregon, and constitutes an important item of subsistence with many of the Prairie Indians. It is the most wary, timid, and fleet animal that inhabits the Plains. It is about the size of a small deer, with a heavy coating of coarse, wiry hair, and its flesh is more tender and juicy than that of the deer. It seldom enters a timbered country, but seems to delight in cropping the grass from the elevated swells of the prairies. When disturbed by the traveler, it will circle around him with the speed of the wind, but does not stop until it reaches some prominent position whence it can survey the country on all sides, and nothing seems to escape its keen vision. They will sometimes stand for a long time and look at a man, provided he does not move or go out of sight; but if he goes behind a hill with the intention of passing around and getting nearer to them, he will never find them again in the same place. I have often tried the experiment, and invariably found that, as soon as I went where the antelope could not see me,

CALLING UP ANTELOPES.

he moved off. Their sense of hearing, as well as vision, is very acute, which renders it difficult to stalk them. By taking advantage of the cover afforded in broken ground, the hunter may, by moving slowly and cautiously over the crests of the irregularities in the surface, sometimes approach within rifle range.

The antelope possesses a greater degree of curiosity than any other animal I know of, and will often approach very near a strange object. The experienced hunter, taking advantage of this peculiarity, lies down and secretes himself in the grass, after which he raises his handkerchief, hand, or foot, so as to attract the attention of the animal, and thus often succeeds in beguiling him within shooting distance.

In some valleys near the Rocky Mountains, where the pasturage is good during the winter season, they collect in immense herds. The Indians are in the habit of surrounding them in such localities and running them with their horses until they tire them out, when they slay large numbers.

The antelope makes a track much shorter than the deer, very broad and round at the heel, and quite sharp at the toe; a little experience renders it easy to distinguish them.

THE BEAR.

Besides the common black bear of the Eastern States, several others are found in the mountains of California, Oregon, Utah, and New Mexico, viz., the grizzly, brown, and cinnamon varieties; all have nearly the same habits, and are hunted in the same manner.

From all I had heard of the grizzly bear, I was induced to believe him one of the most formidable and savage animals in the universe, and that the man who would deliberately encounter and kill one of these beasts had performed a signal feat of courage which entitled him to a lofty position among the votaries of Nimrod. So firmly had I become impressed with this conviction, that I should have been very reluctant to fire upon one had I met him when alone and on foot. The grizzly bear is assuredly the monarch of the American forests, and, so far as physical strength is concerned, he is perhaps without a rival in the world; but, after some experience in hunting, my opinions regarding his courage and his willingness to attack men have very materially changed.

In passing over the elevated tablelands lying between the two forks of the Platte River in 1858, I encountered a full-grown female grizzly bear, with two cubs, very quietly reposing upon the open prairie, several miles distant from any timber. This being the first opportunity that had ever occurred to me for an encounter with the ursine monster, and being imbued with the most exalted notions of the beast's proclivities for offensive warfare, especially when in the presence of her offspring, it may very justly be imagined that I was rather more excited than usual. I, however, determined to make the assault. I felt the utmost confidence in my horse, as she was afraid of nothing; and, after arranging everything about my saddle and arms in good order, I advanced to within about eighty yards before I was discovered by the bear, when she raised upon her haunches and gave me a scrutinizing examination. I seized this opportune moment to fire, but missed my aim, and she started off, followed by her cubs at their utmost speed. After reloading my rifle, I pursued, and, on coming again within range, delivered another shot, which struck the large bear in the fleshy part of the thigh, whereupon she set up a most distressing howl and accelerated her pace, leaving her cubs behind. After loading again I gave the spurs to my horse and resumed the chase, soon passing the cubs, who were making the most plaintive cries of distress. They were heard by the dam, but she gave no other heed to them than occasionally to halt for an instant, turn around, sit up on her posteriors, and give a hasty look back; but, as soon as she saw me following her, she invariably turned again and redoubled her speed. I pursued about four miles and fired four balls into her before I succeeded in bringing her to the ground and from the time I first saw her until her death wound, notwithstanding I was often very close upon her heels, she never came to bay or made the slightest demonstration of resistance. Her sole purpose seemed to be to make her escape, leaving her cubs in the most cowardly manner.

Upon three other different occasions I met the mountain bears, and once the cinnamon species, which is called the most formidable of all, and in none of these instances did they exhibit the slightest indication of anger or resistance, but invariably ran from me.

Such is my experience with this formidable monarch of the mountains. It is possible that if a man came suddenly upon the beast in a thicket, where it could have no previous warning, he might be attacked; but it is my opinion that if the bear gets the wind or sight of a man at any considerable distance, it will endeavor to get away as soon as possible. I am so fully impressed with this idea that I shall hereafter hunt bear with a feeling of as much security as I would have in hunting the buffalo.

The grizzly, like the black bear, hibernates in winter, and makes his appearance in the spring with his claws grown out long and very soft and tender; he is then poor, and unfit for food.

I have heard a very curious fact stated by several old mountaineers regarding the mountain bears, which, of course, I cannot vouch for, but it is given by them with great apparent sincerity and candor. They assert that no instance has ever been known of a female bear having been killed in a state of pregnancy. This singular fact in the history of the animal seems most inexplicable to me, unless she remain concealed in her brumal slumber until after she has been delivered of her cubs.

I was told by an old Delaware Indian that when

the bear has been traveling against the wind and wishes to lie down, he always turns in an opposite direction, and goes some distance away from his first track before making his bed. If an enemy then comes upon his trail, his keen sense of smell will apprise him of the danger. The same Indian mentioned that when a bear had been pursued and sought shelter in a cave, he had often endeavored to eject him with smoke, but that the bear would advance to the mouth of the cave, where the fire was burning, and put it out with his paws, then retreat into the cave again. This would indicate that Bruin is endowed with some glimpses of reason beyond the ordinary instincts of the brute creation in general, and, indeed, is capable of discerning the connection between cause and effect. Notwithstanding the extraordinary intelligence which this quadruped exhibits upon some occasions, upon others he shows himself to be one of the most stupid brutes imaginable. For example, when he has taken possession of a cavern, and the courageous hunter enters with a torch and rifle, it is said he will, instead of forcibly ejecting the intruder, raise himself upon his haunches and cover his eyes with his paws, so as to exclude the light, apparently thinking that in this situation he cannot be seen. The hunter can then approach as close as he pleases and shoot him down.

THE BIGHORN.

The bighorn or mountain sheep, which has a body like the deer, with the head of a sheep, surmounted by an enormous pair of short, heavy horns, is found throughout the Rocky Mountains, and resorts to the most inaccessible peaks and to the wildest and least-frequented glens. It clambers over almost perpendicular cliffs with the greatest ease and celerity, and skips from rock to rock, cropping the tender herbage that grows upon them.

It has been supposed by some that this animal leaps down from crag to crag, lighting upon his horns, as an evidence of which it has been advanced that the front part of the horns is often much battered. This I believe to be erroneous, as it is very common to see horns that have no bruises upon them.

The old mountaineers say they have often seen the bucks engaged in desperate encounters with their huge horns, which, in striking together, made loud reports. This will account for the marks sometimes seen upon them.

The flesh of the bighorn, when fat, is more tender, juicy, and delicious than that of any other animal I know of, but it is a *bon bouche* which will not grace the tables of our city epicures until a railroad to the Rocky Mountains affords the means of transporting it to a market a thousand miles distant from its haunts.

In its habits the mountain sheep greatly resembles the chamois of Switzerland, and it is hunted in the same manner. The hunter traverses the most inaccessible and broken localities, moving along with great caution, as the least unusual noise causes them to flit away like a phantom, and they will be seen no more. The animal is gregarious, but it is seldom that more than eight or ten are found in a flock. When not grazing they seek the sheltered sides of the mountains, and repose among the rocks.